AF674956

Biblical Theology of Missions

Israel and the Nations

Volume 3

Dr. Venkat Potana

Biblical Theology of Missions:

Israel and the Nations

Volume-3

Potana Publications

An imprint of COACH Trust

Dr. Venkat Potana

Copyright

© 2019 by Dr. Venkat Potana
All rights reserved.

No part of this publication may be reproduced, stored in a retrieval system, or transmitted in any form or by any means electronic, mechanical, photocopying, recording, or otherwise without the prior written permission of the publisher, except for brief quotations used in critical reviews or scholarly works.

Title: **Biblical Theology of Missions:** ***Israel and the Nations,*** **Volume-3**

Author: Dr. Venkat Potana

ISBN: 978-81-686654-3-9

Publication Date: 23/01/2019

Product Composition: Single-component retail product
Language: English

Christian Outreach And Compassionate Help

Potana Publications: *An Imprint of COACH Trust*

For permissions or correspondence, please contact:
potanabooks@gmail.com

Foreword

Biblical Theology of Missions: Israel and the Nations, Volume-3 by Dr. Venkat Potana stands as a carefully woven exploration of one of Scripture's most profound movements: the shaping of a people whose identity is continuously formed in relation to divine purpose and the nations of the world. This volume does not merely recount Israel's historical journey; it interprets it as a dynamic theological movement where calling, covenant, redemption, and disruption converge into a single unfolding narrative. Dr. Potana's work brings clarity to a complex storyline, showing how each stage of Israel's experience carries forward an intentional progression rather than isolated historical events.

What makes this work particularly significant is its ability to hold together depth and readability without sacrificing either. Dr. Potana traces the development from covenant formation to exile with a steady interpretive lens that keeps mission at the center of the biblical text. The writing does not reduce the story into abstraction, nor does it flatten its theological richness. Instead, it draws the reader into the lived tension of identity formation, where divine calling is continuously engaged by human history, institutional development, and cultural interaction. The result is a narrative that feels both academically grounded and devotionally resonant, offering insight that speaks to both mind and reflection.

This volume also serves as a vital bridge within the larger series, preparing the conceptual and theological space for what follows in the unfolding of redemptive fulfillment. Dr. Venkat Potana's work carefully positions Israel not as the endpoint of mission, but as a formative stage within a wider divine movement that continues to expand beyond geographic, political, and historical boundaries. It is this forward-facing vision that gives the book its lasting value, inviting readers to see mission not as a static doctrine, but as a living trajectory carried through history itself.

— Rev. Jonathan R. Caldwell

About the Book

Biblical Theology of Missions: Israel and the Nations, Volume-3 by Dr. Venkat Potana offers a rare synthesis of biblical narrative, theological depth, and historical movement, tracing how Israel's identity is shaped through covenant, crisis, and continuity. This volume carefully unfolds the journey from redemption to exile, showing how divine purpose is carried not only through moments of triumph but also through instability, institutional change, and cultural displacement. Dr. Potana's writing brings coherence to the vast sweep of Scripture, allowing readers to see how mission is not an added theme but the underlying movement of the entire biblical story.

What sets this work apart is its ability to speak with both clarity and depth while maintaining a deeply engaging narrative flow. Dr. Venkat Potana does not treat Scripture as fragmented history but as a unified unfolding of divine intention that moves through Israel toward the nations and beyond. Readers are drawn into a compelling interpretive vision where identity, geography, leadership, worship, and prophetic voice all converge into one continuous story of mission in motion. This is not only a study of Israel's past, but an invitation to see how that past shapes a far-reaching vision of purpose that continues to echo through history, making this volume an essential read for anyone seeking a serious and transformative understanding of biblical mission.

Dedication

To my wife, Rita Roslin Potana, my love,

You have been God's gift to my life, my closest companion, and my constant source of strength and joy. Through every season, your faith, patience, and quiet wisdom have shaped my heart and steadied my calling. Your love has taught me what covenant truly means, and your presence has made every journey richer and more meaningful.

This book is written with gratitude for the life we share, the love we nurture, and the faith we live together. You are my blessing, my partner, and my enduring song of grace.

— Dr. Venkat Potana

Contents

Preface

The biblical story does not begin with institutions, nor does it end with them. It begins with a voice that calls, a promise that unfolds, and a history that gradually becomes the stage upon which divine intention is revealed. Within this unfolding movement, Israel emerges not as a self-contained subject of study, but as a people formed, reshaped, and carried through successive transformations of identity, geography, crisis, and hope. *Biblical Theology of Missions: Israel and the Nations, Volume-3* is written with this movement in view, seeking to trace how mission is not an added theme within Scripture, but the very current through which its narrative flows.

This volume follows Israel through covenant formation, redemption, wilderness formation, settlement in the land, emergence of monarchy, prophetic interruption, and eventual dispersion into exile. Each stage is approached not as an isolated historical unit, but as part of a continuous theological trajectory in which calling and history remain inseparably linked. The intention throughout this work is to read Scripture as a unified story of divine engagement with humanity, where identity is never static and purpose is never confined to a single stage of development. In doing so, the reader is invited to observe how divine purpose persists even when human structures shift, fracture, or fail.

The approach adopted here is intentionally narrative and reflective, drawing together theological insight and lived historical movement without reducing either. It seeks to present Israel's journey as both deeply particular and broadly significant, where the unfolding of one people becomes a window into a wider horizon of divine concern for the nations. As the chapters progress, attention is given to how identity is formed not only through moments of clarity and stability, but also through displacement, tension, and reinterpretation. This tension becomes the very space in which meaning is carried forward.

It is my hope that readers will not approach this volume merely as a study of ancient history, but as an invitation to follow a story still in motion. The narrative it traces is not closed, nor does it conclude within its own boundaries. Instead, it opens outward, preparing the ground for further exploration of how this unfolding mission finds its fulfillment beyond Israel while remaining deeply rooted in it. May this work serve as a careful guide into that larger horizon where history, theology, and mission converge into one continuing story.

CHAPTER 1 — ABRAHAM AND THE MISSIONAL CALL

The narrative of mission in Scripture does not begin with systems, nations, or institutions, but with a single voice addressing a single life. Abraham stands at the threshold of this movement, not as a figure defined by achievement, but as one summoned into uncertainty by promise. His calling marks the beginning of a trajectory where divine intention is no longer confined to scattered hints within history, but begins to take shape through a directed life that carries meaning beyond itself. In this moment, departure becomes more than relocation; it becomes the first visible expression of a purpose that extends outward from the personal into the historical.

This chapter explores how that initial summons establishes a pattern that will echo throughout the biblical narrative. Abraham's journey is not presented as an isolated act of obedience, but as the foundation of a larger unfolding in which blessing is never meant to terminate upon the individual, but to move through him toward others. Within this calling, land, identity, and future are all placed into motion, revealing that mission is embedded at the very origin of the story. What begins here is not simply the story of a patriarch, but the shaping of a people whose existence is defined by movement toward purpose that has not yet fully revealed itself.

Call and Departure

The beginning of Abraham's story marks a decisive shift in the Bible where God engages a single life in order to open a wider path for humanity. The movement here grows out of a world already shaped by dispersion, yet it now gathers direction through one person. Calling and movement come together in this moment. The call is a living word that leads to action. From this point onward, mission begins to take visible form through a life that responds to God's voice with trust and obedience.

Divine voice

The narrative opens with a direct and personal address: "Go from your country and your kindred and your father's house to the land that I will show you" (Genesis 12:1). This voice enters Abraham's life with clarity and authority. God speaks, and in that speaking, a new future begins. The Bible presents this moment as a turning point where divine initiative reshapes human direction.

This voice does more than instruct. It creates relationship. Abraham is drawn into a journey where God's presence becomes central. Later reflection affirms this moment as divine revelation: "The God of glory appeared to our father Abraham" (Acts 7:2). The origin of this movement rests in God, who makes Himself known and invites a human life into His purpose.

Interrupted life

Before this call, Abraham's life reflects continuity within family, land, and inherited identity. These structures provide stability and meaning. The call of God enters this settled world and redirects it. The instruction to leave country, people, and household reaches into the deepest layers of belonging.

This redirection reshapes life at its core. Abraham does not continue his previous path with small adjustments. His life now moves in a new direction defined by God's word. The call opens a future that will be formed through trust. As Hebrews reflects, he "went out, not knowing where he was going" (Hebrews 11:8). The interruption becomes the beginning of a journey shaped by promise rather than certainty.

Leaving as response

The Bible presents Abraham's response with striking simplicity: "So Abram went, as the Lord had told him" (Genesis 12:4). This brief statement carries deep meaning. Abraham responds through action. His movement reveals trust in the one who has spoken.

Leaving becomes more than physical relocation. It expresses alignment with divine direction. Abraham steps into a new identity shaped by obedience. His life is now directed by calling rather than by origin. Faith becomes visible through response. It takes form in movement, in decisions, and in willingness to follow God beyond what is already known.

This moment sets a pattern. When God calls, response leads to movement. Abraham's departure becomes the first expression of a life shaped by trust and guided by divine purpose.

Unmapped journey

The destination is described in open terms: "to the land that I will show you" (Genesis 12:1). The promise is clear, yet the details remain hidden at the beginning. Abraham moves forward without a defined map. His journey unfolds step by step.

This shapes the inner life. It creates dependence on God in each stage. Abraham cannot rely on full knowledge of the future. He learns to trust the presence of God who leads him. The journey becomes a place of formation. Each step deepens his relationship with God.

Walking without full clarity does not weaken the call. It strengthens trust. Abraham's life shows that direction comes through relationship, not through complete information.

From place to purpose

As Abraham continues, a transformation takes place. His identity shifts from being rooted in place to being shaped by purpose. The call lifts his life into a wider horizon. What began as a personal journey now carries meaning that extends far beyond him.

God's words reveal this expanding purpose: "I will make of you a great nation, and I will bless you… so that you will be a blessing" (Genesis 12:2). His life becomes part of a movement that reaches outward. Through Abraham, a path opens toward others.

This moment stands as a recognized turning point in biblical theology. As one scholar observes, "The call of Abram is a turning point in the book of Genesis."[1] Abraham becomes the beginning of a directed history in which God works through a person for the sake of many.

The story speaks with clarity even today. God calls, and lives are reshaped. A single step of obedience opens into a journey filled with purpose. Abraham's departure becomes the beginning of a life guided by God and connected to a larger plan.

---

[1] Gordon J. Wenham, *Genesis 1–15*, Word Biblical Commentary, vol. 1 (Waco, TX: Word Books, 1987), 272.

Promise and Direction

The journey that begins with Abraham's departure does not move forward in silence. It is sustained and shaped by promise. The Bible presents this promise as the thread that holds the journey together. Abraham walks without a map, yet he does not walk without direction. What guides him is the word that God has spoken. That word carries within it a future, and that future begins to define his present. Promise becomes the quiet force that gives meaning to every step he takes.

Forward pull

When God speaks to Abraham, the words are filled with forward movement: "I will make of you a great nation, and I will bless you… and in you all the families of the earth shall be blessed" (Genesis 12:2–3). These words do not describe what Abraham already sees. They describe what lies ahead. The promise pulls him forward into a reality that is still forming.

This forward pull shapes how Abraham lives. He does not measure his life only by what is visible in the moment. He carries within him a sense of what God will do. This changes how he walks, how he waits, and how he endures. The promise becomes like a light ahead on a long road. It does not remove the distance, yet it gives reason to continue.

In many lives, direction often comes from immediate results. Abraham's journey reveals another pattern. Direction comes from what God has spoken about the future. Even when the present feels incomplete, the promise continues to guide.

Land and lineage

Two elements stand at the center of God's promise to Abraham: land and lineage. God says, "To your offspring I will give this land" (Genesis 12:7). At this moment, Abraham owns nothing of what is promised. He walks through the land as a stranger. Yet the promise declares that this place will one day be connected to his descendants.

Lineage carries the same tension. Abraham has no child at this stage. The promise of becoming a great nation seems distant. Yet God speaks as if the future is already certain. Abraham begins to live with this tension between what is seen and what is promised.

This tension shapes his journey. It teaches him to hold on to what God has said even when circumstances do not yet reflect it. The land is before him, yet not possessed. The future is spoken, yet not fulfilled. In this space, Abraham learns to trust the faithfulness of God.

A similar pattern can be seen in the life of a young teacher in South Asia who felt called to serve in a remote village. The place had no established church, no visible support, and very little response at the beginning. For several years, his work seemed to produce little change. Yet he continued because he carried a sense of direction that did not come from results but from conviction. Over time, small gatherings began, relationships formed, and a community slowly took shape. The promise did not arrive all at once. It unfolded through steady faithfulness. Abraham's journey reflects this same rhythm.

Identity shaped

As Abraham continues, the promise begins to shape who he is. His identity is no longer formed only by his past or his surroundings. It is formed by what God has spoken over his life. He becomes a person who lives in response to promise.

This shaping can be seen in moments where Abraham builds altars and calls on the name of the Lord (Genesis 12:8). These acts reflect a life oriented toward God. The promise does not remain an idea. It becomes part of Abraham's daily existence. It shapes his decisions, his movements, and his relationship with God.

Identity formed through promise carries a quiet strength. It does not depend on immediate success or visible confirmation. It grows through trust in what God has said. Abraham's life shows that when God speaks, that word has the power to form a person from within.

Open horizon

The promise given to Abraham carries an open horizon. It speaks of a future that extends beyond his lifetime. The blessing is described in terms that reach toward all families of the earth (Genesis 12:3). This gives Abraham's journey a sense of expansion. His life becomes connected to something far greater than his immediate experience.

This open horizon means that the promise cannot be contained within a single moment. It unfolds across time. Abraham begins the journey, yet its full meaning will continue beyond him. This creates a sense of participation in something ongoing.

Living with an open horizon requires patience. It invites a person to trust that God's work continues even when the full picture is not yet visible. Abraham walks with this awareness. His journey becomes part of a larger story that is still moving forward.

Steady ground

While the promise points forward, it also provides stability. Abraham lives in uncertainty, moving from place to place, facing situations that test his trust. Yet within all this movement, the promise remains constant. It becomes the steady ground beneath his steps.

God reaffirms this promise in different moments, strengthening Abraham's confidence. In Genesis 15:5, God brings him outside and says, "Look toward heaven, and number the stars… so shall your offspring be." This image gives Abraham something to hold on to. The promise is repeated, not because God forgets, but because human hearts need reassurance.

Stability within uncertainty becomes one of the most powerful aspects of Abraham's journey. His circumstances change, yet the promise remains. This allows him to continue even when the path is unclear.

A recent account tells of a family who relocated to a region affected by conflict to serve displaced communities. Their environment shifted often, and their plans required constant adjustment. Yet they held on to a clear sense of purpose that guided their decisions. Over time, they saw lives restored, children educated, and communities rebuilt. Their stability did not come from their surroundings. It came from a deeper conviction that gave direction through uncertainty. Abraham's journey reflects this same kind of steady ground.

The promise of God continues to work in this way. It draws forward, shapes identity, opens horizons, and provides stability. Abraham's life shows that promise is not only about what will happen in the future. It becomes the guiding force of the present. Through it, a life is directed, sustained, and connected to a purpose that continues to unfold.

As one scholar notes, "The promises to Abraham are the foundation of the subsequent history of Israel,"[2] highlighting how this moment carries enduring significance far beyond Abraham's own journey.

Blessing and Extension

The promise spoken over Abraham does not end with him. From the beginning, it carries movement within it. God says, "I will bless you… so that you will be a blessing… and in you all the families of the earth shall be blessed" (Genesis 12:2–3). These words open a wider horizon. Blessing is received, yet it does not remain contained. It begins to move outward. Abraham stands at the starting point of a flow that reaches beyond his own life.

Given to be shared

When God blesses Abraham, He does not speak only about what Abraham will gain. The blessing carries purpose. It is given in such a way that it can be shared. Abraham becomes a channel through which something greater passes to others.

This changes how blessing is understood. It is not a private possession. It is relational. It touches one life and then continues its movement. Abraham begins to see that what he receives from God connects him to others. His journey is no longer about himself alone. It becomes a pathway through which others will experience the goodness of God.

In one village in Southeast Asia, a small group of women began meeting weekly to pray for their families. They faced economic hardship and limited opportunity, yet they chose to gather and support one another. Over time, they started helping widows in their community with food and small income projects. Their own lives were still modest, yet something began to flow through them. What they had received in encouragement and faith began to reach others. The blessing did not stay within their circle. It extended outward in quiet and steady ways. Abraham's story reflects this same movement.

---

[2] R. W. L. Moberly, "The Earliest Commentary on the Akedah," *Vetus Testamentum* 38, no. 3 (1988): 302.

Beyond the self

As Abraham walks with God, the promise continues to expand. The words spoken over him include "all the families of the earth" (Genesis 12:3). This brings a shift in perspective. Abraham's life is connected to people he will never meet. His journey carries meaning that reaches far beyond his immediate surroundings.

This expansion invites a different way of living. Abraham cannot think only in terms of his own needs or achievements. He begins to carry a sense of responsibility toward others. The blessing he has received places him within a larger purpose. His life becomes part of a story that includes many.

This movement beyond the self can be seen in moments where Abraham interacts with others. In Genesis 13, when conflict arises between his herdsmen and Lot's, Abraham chooses peace. He allows Lot to choose the land first. This action reflects a heart shaped by blessing. He does not grasp for advantage. He lives with a sense that God's promise provides enough. His actions begin to reflect the character of the God who has called him.

Carried through a life

Blessing does not move outward automatically. It is carried through the life of the one who receives it. Abraham becomes the place where this movement takes shape. His decisions, his relationships, and his responses all become part of how blessing reaches others.

In Genesis 14, Abraham rescues Lot and the people taken captive. After this, he meets Melchizedek, who blesses him and gives thanks to God (Genesis 14:19–20). In this moment, blessing is both received and recognized. It flows through Abraham's actions and becomes visible in the lives of others.

This shows that blessing involves participation. It is not passive. Abraham lives in such a way that what God has given begins to touch those around him. His life becomes a meeting point where divine intention and human response come together.

A young doctor in a rural region of East Africa once shared how she began her work with very limited resources. She treated patients under a tree before a small clinic was built. Over time, her consistent care drew others to join the work. Nurses came, volunteers assisted, and a small hospital eventually developed. What began as one person's commitment became a place where many received help and hope. The blessing did not remain with her. It moved through her into a wider community. Abraham's life reflects this same pattern of lived extension.

From one to many

The movement of blessing in Abraham's life follows a clear direction. It begins with one person and moves toward many. God's words hold this direction from the start. The promise is personal, yet its goal is wide.

This movement can be seen in how God continues to reaffirm the promise. In Genesis 18:18, God says that Abraham "shall surely become a great and mighty nation, and all the nations of the earth shall be blessed in him." The language expands. The scope grows. The blessing continues to move outward.

This direction shapes how Abraham understands his place in the world. He is part of something that is growing. His life contributes to a future that will include many people and nations. The blessing carries within it a sense of multiplication.

Living movement

Blessing in Abraham's story is never still. It moves, it grows, and it reaches outward. It begins with God, passes through Abraham, and continues toward others. This movement gives life to the promise. It shows that what God gives is meant to flow.

For those who read this story, the same pattern becomes visible. Blessing is received in order to be shared. It takes shape in relationships, in actions, and in choices that reflect God's goodness. A life touched by God becomes a place where others can also encounter His grace.

Abraham's journey reveals that blessing is dynamic. It carries movement within it. It begins with one life, yet it does not end there. It continues to extend, reaching outward and drawing others into its flow. As one scholar notes, "the promise to Abraham is intrinsically expansive, embracing others beyond himself,"[3] capturing the outward direction that defines this moment in the Bible.

---

[3] Daniel J. Estes, "Looking for Abraham's Blessing: A Study in the Concept of Blessing in Genesis," *Bibliotheca Sacra* 168, no. 669 (2011): 27.

Faith as Participation

The promise given to Abraham does not remain outside of him. It calls for a response that enters into the very movement of God. Faith becomes the way Abraham lives within that movement. It is not presented as a single moment or a fixed statement. It unfolds across time, shaping how he walks, how he waits, and how he responds. The Bible describes this with quiet depth: "And he believed the Lord, and he counted it to him as righteousness" (Genesis 15:6). This belief is not distant or abstract. It becomes the thread that holds Abraham's life together as he continues in the path opened before him.

Trust unfolding

Abraham's faith does not appear fully formed at the beginning. It grows as the promise unfolds. When God first calls him, Abraham responds by going. Later, when the promise seems delayed, he wrestles with questions. In Genesis 15:2, he asks, "O Lord God, what will you give me, for I continue childless?" This moment reveals something real and human. Faith does not remove questions. It carries them into relationship with God.

God responds by reaffirming the promise and inviting Abraham to look at the stars: "So shall your offspring be" (Genesis 15:5). In that moment, Abraham chooses to trust again. His faith moves forward, even when the present situation has not changed. Trust becomes something that unfolds step by step. It is renewed as God speaks and as Abraham responds.

This unfolding trust can be seen in the life of a young pastor who began serving in an urban settlement where people were constantly moving in and out. Relationships were fragile, and continuity was difficult. At times, it felt as if nothing lasting could be built. Yet he continued to invest in people, one conversation at a time. Years later, small groups formed, and a sense of community began to emerge. His journey did not follow a straight line. Trust grew through seasons of uncertainty. Abraham's path reflects this same rhythm.

Lived alignment

Faith in Abraham's life takes visible form. It is expressed in the way he aligns his actions with what God has said. When he builds altars, when he calls on the name of the Lord, when he moves according to God's direction, his faith becomes part of his daily life (Genesis 12:7–8).

This alignment does not come from perfect understanding. It comes from a willingness to walk with God. Abraham's decisions begin to reflect the relationship he has entered. His life shows that faith is not limited to inward belief. It is lived out through choices that follow God's voice.

This kind of alignment can be seen wherever people shape their lives around a sense of calling. A teacher who chooses to remain in a difficult school, a nurse who continues to serve in a demanding environment, a worker who acts with integrity when shortcuts seem easier—these are quiet expressions of faith. They reflect lives that are aligned with something deeper than immediate comfort. Abraham's story invites this kind of lived response.

Shared journey

Faith also means entering into what God is doing. Abraham does not stand outside the promise as an observer. He becomes a participant. His life is woven into the unfolding of God's purpose. This participation brings both moments of clarity and moments of testing.

In Genesis 22, when Abraham is called to offer Isaac, his faith reaches a profound depth. The promise and the command seem to stand in tension. Yet Abraham moves forward, trusting that God remains faithful. The Bible later reflects on this moment by saying that Abraham considered that God was able even to raise the dead (Hebrews 11:19). His faith engages the promise even when the path becomes difficult.

Participation means that faith involves risk, trust, and surrender. Abraham's life shows that walking with God includes moments where understanding feels limited. Yet in those moments, faith continues to hold on to who God is.

Steady through change

Abraham's journey includes many changes. He moves from place to place, faces challenges, and experiences delays in the fulfillment of the promise. Through all of this, faith provides continuity. It becomes the steady thread that runs through changing circumstances.

In Genesis 13, after a time in Egypt, Abraham returns to the place where he had first built an altar and calls again on the name of the Lord (Genesis 13:4). This return reflects continuity in his relationship with God. Even when circumstances shift, his faith brings him back to the center of that relationship.

This steady quality of faith can be seen in lives that continue through long seasons without visible results. A group working among displaced communities in a coastal region continued their efforts for years with limited progress. Gradually, trust developed, and opportunities for deeper engagement opened. Their work did not depend on quick outcomes. It was sustained by a steady commitment. Abraham's journey reflects this same kind of endurance.

Relationship in action

At its heart, Abraham's faith is relational. It grows out of his connection with God and shapes how he acts. His obedience, his trust, and his decisions all flow from this relationship. Faith becomes the way he lives with God in the unfolding of the promise.

This relationship shapes his actions in ways that affect others. His choices reflect a trust that allows him to act with generosity, patience, and courage. Faith is not separated from life. It becomes the way life is lived in response to God.

As one scholar observes, "Abraham's faith is not mere assent but active trust expressed in obedience."[4] This captures the heart of his journey. Faith moves beyond words. It becomes participation in what God is doing.

Abraham's story shows that faith is a path, not a single step. It grows through trust, takes shape in action, and continues through changing seasons. It allows a person to walk within the movement of God, holding on to His promise while living in the present. Through faith, Abraham becomes part of a story that continues to unfold, step by step, under the guidance of God.

Nations in View

As Abraham continues to walk with God, the horizon of his calling becomes wider. What began as a personal journey now

---

[4] John J. Collins, "Faith and Obedience in the Abraham Narrative," *Catholic Biblical Quarterly* 52, no. 2 (1990): 218.

opens toward the whole human family. The words spoken at the beginning continue to echo with growing clarity: "in you all the families of the earth shall be blessed" (Genesis 12:3). This statement places Abraham's life within a global frame. His steps are local, yet their meaning reaches far beyond the places he travels. The promise carries within it a vision that gathers the nations into view.

Beyond the immediate

Abraham lives in a particular land, among particular people, and within specific moments. Yet the promise constantly stretches beyond what is immediate. It speaks of "families of the earth," a phrase that brings distant peoples into the picture. Abraham's life is connected to those he has never seen.

This changes the way his journey is understood. It is not limited to his personal story. It becomes part of a movement that includes many. The blessing that flows through him is meant to reach outward. The call, the promise, and the faith he carries all move toward a wider horizon.

In one coastal region of South Asia, a small fellowship began among fishermen who gathered after long days at sea. Over time, visitors from nearby communities joined them, drawn by the sense of hope and unity they experienced. What began in a small circle slowly connected people across different villages and backgrounds. The movement grew beyond its original setting. In a quiet way, the lives of many became linked through something that started with a few. Abraham's story reflects this same outward movement.

Within the promise

The nations are not an afterthought. They are present within the promise from the beginning. When God speaks to Abraham, the language already includes a wider world. The promise does not move from small to large by accident. It carries expansion within its structure.

This can be seen again when God speaks in Genesis 18:18: "all the nations of the earth shall be blessed in him." The words return with strength and clarity. They show that Abraham's life stands within a plan that reaches toward all people. The promise holds together the particular and the universal. One life becomes the starting point for a movement that touches many.

This understanding brings depth to Abraham's journey. His actions, his decisions, and his faith all take place within a story that includes the nations. Even when he walks alone, he carries a future that involves others.

Widening scope

As the narrative moves forward, the scope continues to widen. Abraham's encounters begin to reflect this. In Genesis 14, he interacts with kings and peoples beyond his immediate circle. In Genesis 20, he finds himself in the land of Gerar, among a different community. His life crosses boundaries and connects with others.

These moments show that the journey is not confined. It moves outward, touching different spaces and relationships. The promise draws Abraham into a wider engagement with the world. His path becomes a place where different peoples intersect.

A recent account tells of a group of young professionals who began meeting in a large city in East Asia. They came from different regions, spoke different languages, and worked in various fields. What brought them together was a shared sense of purpose rooted in faith. Over time, their network extended into other cities and countries. Their connections grew, and their influence reached beyond their original setting. What began as a local gathering became part of a wider movement. Abraham's journey reflects this same widening scope.

One line, many lives

The promise given to Abraham moves through a particular line, yet its effect reaches many lives. This creates a connection between one and many. Abraham stands as a starting point, yet the direction always moves outward.

This pattern shows how God works within history. He begins with one life, shapes it through calling and promise, and then allows that life to become a channel through which others are reached. The focus remains clear, yet the impact expands.

This movement from one to many does not diminish the importance of the individual. It deepens it. Abraham's life gains meaning as it becomes connected to a larger purpose. His journey becomes part of something that continues beyond him.

Toward future engagement

The nations in view point toward a future that is still unfolding. Abraham does not see the full realization of what has been promised. Yet he walks with an awareness that his life contributes to that future. The direction is set, even when the destination remains ahead.

This orientation toward future engagement gives his journey a sense of purpose that extends beyond the present moment. Each step becomes part of a larger story. The promise continues to move forward, carrying the hope of connection and blessing for many.

As one scholar notes, "the Abrahamic promise has a universal horizon that embraces the nations."[5] This insight captures the direction that shapes Abraham's calling. His life stands at the beginning of a movement that reaches outward, gathering people into its flow.

For those who follow this story, the same horizon comes into view. Life is not limited to personal experience. It becomes part of a wider purpose that includes others. Abraham's journey shows that when God calls one life, He often has many in view. The path may begin in a single place, yet it opens toward the world.

---

[5] Richard S. Hess, "The Genealogies of Genesis 1–11 and Comparative Literature," *Biblica* 70, no. 2 (1989): 254.

CHAPTER 2 — COVENANT AND ELECTED PURPOSE

The movement that begins with Abraham's calling does not remain open-ended or undefined for long. It gradually takes shape through covenant, where promise is no longer only spoken but formally established within a binding relational framework. In this transition, divine intention moves from initiation into structure, giving continuity to what has been set in motion. Covenant becomes the space where calling is clarified, not as possession of privilege, but as participation in a purpose that is sustained through relationship, responsibility, and endurance across time.

Within this framework, election is not presented as separation for its own sake, but as direction toward function. The chosen identity of Abraham's descendants begins to carry weight beyond itself, forming a community positioned within history for a role that extends outward. This chapter traces how covenant shapes identity into responsibility, and how election redefines belonging as engagement with a larger mission. What emerges is a structured continuity between promise and purpose, where identity is no longer only received, but also lived through faithful participation in what God intends to accomplish through history.

Covenant Formation

The journey that began with Abraham stepping into the unknown now reaches a moment of deep settling. The voice that called him, the promise that guided him, now takes on a clearer and stronger form. God does not leave Abraham walking with uncertainty alone. He draws near and establishes something firm, something lasting. This moment is described in the Bible as covenant. It is here that movement becomes relationship, and promise becomes anchored in commitment.

Divine beginning

The covenant does not begin with Abraham's initiative. It begins with God. In Genesis 15, Abraham stands under the open sky, still holding the promise yet still waiting for its fulfillment.

Into that waiting, God speaks again, reassuring him: "Fear not, Abram, I am your shield; your reward shall be very great" (Genesis 15:1). These words carry both protection and assurance. They remind Abraham that the journey is sustained by God Himself.

As the conversation unfolds, God brings Abraham into a moment that is both personal and profound. Abraham prepares the animals as instructed, placing them in order (Genesis 15:9–10). Then something unexpected happens. A deep sleep falls upon him, and in that stillness, God alone passes through the pieces in the form of a smoking fire pot and a flaming torch (Genesis 15:17). The action speaks quietly yet powerfully. God takes the initiative. The covenant rests on His commitment.

This moment reveals the heart of covenant. It is not built on human strength. It is grounded in divine faithfulness. Abraham is invited into something that God Himself establishes and sustains.

Promise secured

The promises spoken earlier now take on a new depth. They are no longer only words that point forward. They are confirmed within this covenant moment. God declares, "To your offspring I give this land" (Genesis 15:18). The promise of land, spoken before, is now sealed within a binding relationship.

This changes how Abraham carries the promise. It is no longer something uncertain or distant. It becomes something secured by God's own action. Even though Abraham still does not possess the land, the promise now has a firmness that holds through time.

In many parts of the world, agreements are often written and signed to ensure trust between people. Yet even those agreements can fail. Here, the covenant goes deeper. It is not simply an agreement. It is a commitment rooted in the character of God. What He speaks, He confirms.

A young leader working among migrant communities once shared how trust was built slowly over years. At first, people listened with hesitation. Promises meant little because they had experienced broken words before. Over time, as consistent care and presence continued, trust began to grow. What made the difference was not many words, but faithful action. In a far greater way, God confirms His promise through covenant. Abraham begins to rest in something that cannot be shaken.

Sign and sealing

The covenant continues to unfold in Genesis 17, where God again speaks to Abraham, saying, “I am God Almighty; walk before me, and be blameless, that I may make my covenant between me and you” (Genesis 17:1–2). Here, the relationship becomes even more defined. God gives a sign, a visible mark that will remain with Abraham and his descendants.

This sign serves as a reminder. It makes the covenant something that touches daily life. It is no longer only a moment in the past. It becomes part of the present. Every time Abraham sees this sign, he remembers that he belongs to a relationship established by God.

The giving of a sign shows that covenant is meant to be lived. It is not distant. It becomes part of identity, shaping how life is understood and lived out.

Nearness of God

One of the most striking aspects of covenant is the nearness it brings. God does not remain distant from Abraham. He draws close. He speaks, reassures, and reveals Himself. In Genesis 17:7, God says, “I will establish my covenant between me and you and your offspring after you… to be God to you and to your offspring after you.” These words carry a deep sense of relationship.

Covenant is not only about what God gives. It is about who God is to His people. Abraham is invited to live with the awareness that God is with him, guiding and sustaining him. This nearness transforms the journey. It brings strength in uncertainty and confidence in waiting.

A family serving in a remote mountainous region once described how isolation marked their early years. Roads were difficult, communication was limited, and support felt distant. Yet over time, they experienced a deep sense of God’s presence in simple and unexpected ways. Their work continued, not because conditions became easier, but because they knew they were not alone. Abraham’s experience reflects this same reality. Covenant brings the assurance of God’s presence within the journey.

Lasting foundation

As Abraham continues, the covenant becomes the foundation of everything that follows. It provides stability across changing circumstances. Abraham still faces challenges. He still waits for fulfillment. Yet the covenant remains constant.

This enduring nature of covenant ensures that the promise does not fade. It carries forward through time. It reaches beyond Abraham to his descendants. It becomes the structure within which God's purpose continues to unfold.

The movement from calling to covenant marks a significant step in the story. What began as a journey now stands on a firm foundation. Abraham is no longer only a traveler guided by promise. He becomes part of a relationship that holds that promise securely.

As one scholar observes, "the covenant in Genesis 15 represents a divine commitment that guarantees the promise independently of human performance."[6] This insight captures the strength of this moment. The covenant rests on God's faithfulness, providing a foundation that endures.

Abraham's life now moves forward with a deeper sense of assurance. The path may still stretch ahead, and the fulfillment may still take time, yet the relationship is secure. Covenant transforms the journey into something rooted, sustained, and carried by the unwavering commitment of God.

Promise and Obligation

The covenant that God establishes with Abraham does more than secure the promise. It also draws Abraham into a way of living that reflects that promise. What God gives and what Abraham does begin to move together. The relationship is not one-sided. God speaks, assures, and commits Himself. Abraham listens, responds, and walks accordingly. In this space, promise and obligation meet. The journey continues, yet now it carries a deeper sense of responsibility shaped by relationship.

Promise reaffirmed

After establishing the covenant, God continues to speak to Abraham, repeating and deepening what has already been

---

[6] Scott W. Hahn, "Covenant in the Old Testament: The Current State of the Question," *Journal for the Study of the Old Testament* 28, no. 3 (2004): 273.

promised. In Genesis 17:4–5, God says, "Behold, my covenant is with you, and you shall be the father of a multitude of nations… your name shall be Abraham." The promise is not withdrawn or weakened. It is strengthened. Even Abraham's name is changed, reflecting the future that God has spoken.

This reaffirmation carries comfort and clarity. Abraham hears again what God intends to do. The promise remains steady even when fulfillment seems delayed. Each time God speaks, the promise is renewed within the covenant.

Yet this repetition also shapes Abraham's awareness. He is reminded that his life now stands within something larger than himself. The promise continues to define his direction. It becomes the anchor that holds him steady as he moves forward.

Shared participation

Alongside the reaffirmed promise, Abraham is invited into active participation. God says, "Walk before me, and be blameless" (Genesis 17:1). This call brings responsibility into the relationship. Abraham is not only a recipient. He becomes a participant.

Participation means that Abraham's daily life matters. His choices, his actions, and his direction all become part of how the covenant is lived out. The relationship with God shapes how he walks. It calls him into a life that reflects trust and alignment.

This kind of participation can be seen in a group of young workers who began serving in an area affected by seasonal flooding. They received support and training from others, yet their work required daily decisions. They organized relief efforts, built relationships, and remained present during difficult times. The help they received became meaningful as they participated actively. In a similar way, Abraham's life becomes the place where covenant is lived.

Obedience expressed

Obedience begins to take visible form within Abraham's journey. When God gives instructions, Abraham responds. In Genesis 17:23, after receiving the covenant sign, Abraham acts "that very day," carrying out what God had spoken. His obedience is immediate and intentional.

This response shows that obedience is not an abstract idea. It is expressed through concrete action. Abraham does not delay or negotiate. He aligns his life with the direction given to him.

Obedience grows out of trust. Abraham believes that what God has spoken is true and reliable. This belief leads him to act. His life becomes a reflection of the relationship he has entered. Each act of obedience strengthens that relationship and deepens his participation within the covenant.

Trust in action

The journey of Abraham includes moments where obedience requires courage. In Genesis 22, when God calls him to offer Isaac, Abraham faces a situation that stretches his understanding. The promise had been connected to Isaac, yet now he is asked to place that promise in God's hands.

Abraham rises early and begins the journey (Genesis 22:3). His actions reveal a deep trust. He moves forward, holding on to the belief that God remains faithful. His faith is not limited to words. It becomes action in the face of uncertainty.

This kind of trust can be seen in the life of a medical team that chose to remain in a region during a sudden outbreak of disease. Many left for safety, yet this group stayed to care for those affected. Their decision came from a deep sense of calling and responsibility. Their trust took shape in action, even when the situation was difficult. Abraham's journey reflects this same pattern of lived trust.

Gift and responsibility

Within the covenant, gift and responsibility remain together. God gives the promise freely. Abraham does not earn it. Yet the gift does not remove responsibility. It calls for a response that reflects the relationship.

This balance becomes clear as the narrative continues. In Genesis 18:19, God speaks of Abraham in these words: "For I have chosen him, that he may command his children and his household after him to keep the way of the Lord by doing righteousness and justice." The covenant reaches into the future, shaping not only Abraham's life but also the lives of those who come after him.

Responsibility grows out of relationship. It does not stand apart from the promise. It flows from it. Abraham's life shows that receiving from God leads to living in a way that reflects Him.

As one scholar notes, "the covenant entails both divine promise and human obligation."[7] This insight captures the balance that defines Abraham's journey. The promise remains secure, yet it calls for a life that responds.

The story continues to move forward with this balance in place. Abraham walks with confidence in what God has promised, and at the same time, he lives with a sense of responsibility shaped by that promise. His journey becomes a living expression of both gift and response, held together within the covenant that God has established.

Election and Function

As the covenant deepens, another layer of meaning begins to emerge. Abraham is not only called and given promise. He is chosen. This choosing carries purpose within it. It does not lift him above others in a way that separates him from them. Instead, it places him within a role that connects him to them. Election becomes the way God directs His work through a particular life for the sake of many.

Chosen within many

Abraham lives in a world filled with people, cultures, and movements. Among all these, God sets His attention on one man and his family. This choice stands out. It is clear, intentional, and purposeful. Yet the moment it happens, it begins to point outward.

God's words already carry this direction: "in you all the families of the earth shall be blessed" (Genesis 12:3). The choosing of Abraham never stands alone. It is tied to a wider horizon. He is selected from among many, yet his life is meant to touch many.

This pattern appears in everyday life as well. A teacher in a crowded city may be given responsibility over a small group of students. The focus rests on those few, yet the purpose extends beyond them. What is shaped in that small group can influence

---

[7] Moshe Weinfeld, "The Covenant of Grant in the Old Testament and in the Ancient Near East," *Journal of the American Oriental Society* 90, no. 2 (1970): 189.

families, neighborhoods, and future paths. In a similar way, Abraham's selection becomes the starting point of something much larger.

Chosen to serve

As Abraham continues his journey, the nature of his calling becomes clearer. Being chosen brings direction. It invites him into a way of living that reflects God's heart. In Genesis 18:19, God speaks about Abraham with these words: "that he may command his children and his household after him to keep the way of the Lord by doing righteousness and justice." This statement reveals purpose. Abraham is chosen to walk in a way that reflects God's character.

This kind of choosing carries responsibility. It calls Abraham to live in a manner that brings life and justice to others. His relationship with God shapes how he relates to people around him. The focus moves from self to service.

In a rural community in East Africa, a group of farmers once received training in sustainable agriculture. They were chosen from among many to begin a new approach. Instead of keeping the knowledge to themselves, they began teaching neighboring villages. Within a few years, entire regions experienced change in food production and stability. Their selection carried responsibility. What they received was meant to be shared. Abraham's calling reflects this same movement.

Place within a larger plan

Election also gives Abraham a place within a story that is still unfolding. His life becomes part of a larger design. God's purpose moves through him, shaping events and opening pathways that will continue beyond his lifetime.

This sense of place becomes clearer as the narrative progresses. God repeatedly affirms that Abraham's descendants will carry forward what has begun (Genesis 17:7–8). The covenant extends, and the purpose continues. Abraham's life stands at the beginning of a line through which God will work in history.

This understanding brings meaning to ordinary moments. Each step Abraham takes, each decision he makes, becomes part of something greater. His journey is no longer isolated. It is connected to a wider movement shaped by God's intention.

Witness among others

Abraham's life does not unfold in isolation. He interacts with different peoples and communities. In these encounters, his relationship with God becomes visible. His actions, his words, and his responses begin to reflect something of the God he serves.

In Genesis 21, when Abraham lives among the Philistines, his presence leads to recognition. Abimelech says to him, "God is with you in all that you do" (Genesis 21:22). This statement shows that Abraham's life has become a witness. Others see the effect of his relationship with God.

This kind of witness does not come through effort to impress. It grows out of a life shaped by God. When Abraham acts with integrity, trust, and peace, those around him begin to notice. His life points beyond itself.

A recent example comes from a small business owner in Southeast Asia who chose to run his company with fairness and care for his employees. Over time, his approach stood out in a competitive environment. Workers from other companies sought employment with him, and conversations began about the values that guided his decisions. His work became a place where others encountered a different way of living. Abraham's life reflects this same quiet witness.

Purpose in motion

Election carries movement within it. It does not remain fixed. It continues to unfold as Abraham walks with God. Each stage of his journey reveals more of the purpose connected to his calling.

The promise, the covenant, and the calling all come together here. Abraham is chosen, yet his life remains open and active. He continues to move, to respond, and to grow within the purpose given to him. His election becomes a living reality.

As one scholar observes, "election in the Old Testament is fundamentally oriented toward service within God's plan for the world."[8] This captures the heart of Abraham's calling. Being chosen places him within a movement that reaches beyond himself.

---

[8] Terence E. Fretheim, "The Book of Genesis," *Interpretation* 50, no. 4 (1996): 347.

The story continues with this understanding. Abraham's life shows that election is not about standing apart. It is about stepping into a role that connects one life to many. Through him, a path opens. Through his journey, others begin to feel the touch of what God is doing.

Identity and Responsibility

As the covenant settles into Abraham's life, something deeper begins to take shape. It is no longer only about where he is going or what he will receive. It begins to answer who he is. The relationship with God forms his identity from within. This identity does not come from land, family background, or surrounding culture. It grows out of belonging to God. From this belonging, a way of living begins to emerge.

Formed by relationship

God's words in Genesis 17:7 carry a strong sense of identity: "I will establish my covenant between me and you and your offspring after you… to be God to you and to your offspring after you." This statement goes beyond promise. It defines relationship. Abraham and his descendants are now a people who belong to God.

This belonging shapes how life is understood. Identity is no longer something constructed from external markers. It is received through relationship. Abraham begins to see himself as one who walks with God, listens to Him, and lives under His direction.

This kind of identity can be seen in the life of a young woman working in a large corporate environment in South Asia. Surrounded by intense competition and pressure, she chose to shape her decisions around integrity and care for others. Over time, colleagues began to recognize a difference in her approach. Her identity did not come from her position or achievements. It came from a deeper sense of who she was before God. Abraham's story reflects this same inward formation.

Distinct way of living

As identity forms, it begins to show itself in daily life. Abraham's journey places him among different peoples and cultures. Yet his life begins to reflect a distinct way of living. This distinctiveness does not come through separation alone. It comes through the values and actions shaped by his relationship with God.

In Genesis 18, Abraham welcomes three visitors with generosity and care. His hospitality reflects a heart formed by relationship. Later in the same chapter, he stands before God and intercedes for the city of Sodom (Genesis 18:23–33). His concern for justice and mercy reveals something of God's own character.

This distinct way of living becomes visible to others. It does not require loud declaration. It is seen in actions, in decisions, and in relationships. Abraham's life begins to carry a quiet difference that reflects the God he serves.

Responsibility in action

Identity brings responsibility. As Abraham understands who he is, he also understands how he is called to live. God speaks of this clearly: "that he may command his children and his household after him to keep the way of the Lord by doing righteousness and justice" (Genesis 18:19). Responsibility is not limited to personal behavior. It extends to how life is guided and passed on.

This responsibility takes shape in everyday actions. It is seen in fairness, in care for others, and in decisions that reflect what is right. Abraham's life becomes a place where these values are practiced.

A group of community leaders in East Africa once worked together to resolve conflicts between neighboring villages. Instead of allowing tension to grow, they chose to bring people together, listen carefully, and seek fair solutions. Their work required patience and courage. Over time, trust began to grow, and relationships were restored. Their actions reflected a sense of responsibility toward others. In a similar way, Abraham's life shows that identity carries a call to act with justice and care.

Life aligned

As Abraham continues his journey, his life becomes increasingly aligned with God's intention. This alignment does not happen in a single moment. It grows through repeated choices to follow God's direction.

When God calls Abraham to move, he moves. When God speaks, he listens. When situations arise, he responds in ways that reflect trust. This alignment shapes the whole of his life. It brings coherence between what he believes and how he lives.

Alignment also brings clarity. Abraham begins to see that his life has direction. It is not driven by circumstances alone. It is guided by relationship with God. This guidance brings stability even when situations change.

Witness through life

As identity and responsibility come together, Abraham's life becomes a witness. Others begin to see the effect of his relationship with God. In Genesis 23, when Abraham negotiates for a burial place, the people of the land say, "You are a prince of God among us" (Genesis 23:6). This recognition shows that his life has made an impression.

This witness does not come from seeking recognition. It grows naturally from a life shaped by God. When Abraham acts with integrity, humility, and faith, those around him notice. His life points beyond itself.

In a coastal city in Southeast Asia, a small group of workers chose to run their daily activities with honesty and fairness in an environment where shortcuts were common. Over time, their approach gained respect. Others began to trust them, and opportunities opened for deeper relationships. Their witness came through consistent conduct. Abraham's life reflects this same quiet influence.

As one scholar notes, "Israel's identity in its earliest form is inseparable from its vocation to embody God's ways."[9] This insight captures what begins in Abraham's story. Identity is not separate from responsibility. It is expressed through it.

The journey continues with this understanding. Abraham is not only called and chosen. He is formed. His identity shapes his responsibility, and his responsibility reflects his identity. Through this, his life becomes a living expression of the covenant, pointing toward the wider purpose that continues to unfold.

Generational Continuity

As the covenant deepens in Abraham's life, its reach begins to stretch beyond him. What God establishes with one man

---

[9] Joel S. Kaminsky, "Election and Ethical Monotheism in the Hebrew Bible," *Journal of Religious Ethics* 31, no. 2 (2003): 220.

does not remain confined to a single lifetime. It carries forward, moving through generations, shaping a people who will continue the journey. The promise is larger than one story. It unfolds across time, linking past, present, and future into one steady movement.

Beyond one life

God's words make this clear: "I will establish my covenant between me and you and your offspring after you throughout their generations for an everlasting covenant" (Genesis 17:7). The covenant is not temporary. It is designed to endure. Abraham becomes the starting point, yet the promise continues beyond him.

This gives a different weight to his journey. His actions are not only for his own life. They carry meaning for those who will come after him. Every step he takes becomes part of a path others will follow. The covenant places his life within a larger timeline.

A schoolteacher in a small town once began teaching children under a tree with very limited resources. She continued year after year, investing in each child who came. Decades later, many of her students became teachers, leaders, and workers who carried forward what they had received. Her influence moved beyond her own years. In a similar way, Abraham's life becomes the beginning of something that continues.

Teaching and remembering

For the covenant to continue, it must be remembered and passed on. God speaks of this responsibility when He says that Abraham will "command his children and his household after him to keep the way of the Lord" (Genesis 18:19). This instruction shows that continuity requires intentional care.

Abraham's role includes guiding the next generation. He becomes a teacher within his own household. The covenant is not preserved by memory alone. It is carried through instruction, conversation, and daily living. What God has done is spoken about, remembered, and lived out again.

This pattern appears wherever values are passed from one generation to another. In a coastal community, a group of elders began gathering young people each week to share stories of resilience, faith, and service. These stories shaped how the younger generation understood their place in the world. Over time, those young people began to carry the same values into their own lives. Abraham's story reflects this same rhythm of teaching and remembering.

Through descendants

The covenant finds its path forward through Abraham's descendants. Isaac, Jacob, and those who follow become part of this unfolding story. Each generation receives what was given before and carries it further.

This continuity does not depend on perfect circumstances. There are moments of struggle, delay, and challenge. Yet the covenant remains steady. It moves through changing situations, holding its direction. The promise continues to guide, even when the journey becomes complex.

In Genesis 26:3–4, God speaks to Isaac, reaffirming the promise given to Abraham. The words echo across generations, showing that the covenant remains active. It is not a memory of the past. It is a living reality that continues to shape the present.

Steady across time

One of the most striking features of the covenant is its stability. Time passes, situations change, and people come and go, yet the covenant holds. It provides a steady foundation that carries through different seasons.

Abraham experiences this stability as he waits for the fulfillment of the promise. Later generations will experience it in their own contexts. The covenant becomes the thread that connects them all.

This steady quality can be seen in the life of a community that faced repeated cycles of hardship due to environmental challenges. Despite these difficulties, they continued to gather, support one another, and hold on to shared values. Over time, their consistency became their strength. What held them together was not ease, but a steady commitment. In a deeper way, the covenant provides this kind of stability for Abraham and his descendants.

Future in view

The covenant always carries a forward direction. It points toward what is yet to come. Abraham does not see the full realization of what has been promised. Yet he walks with the assurance that the future is held within God's commitment.

This future orientation shapes how each generation lives. They are not only looking back at what God has done. They are moving forward into what He will do. The covenant keeps their eyes lifted beyond the present moment.

As one scholar notes, "the Abrahamic covenant is inherently generational, extending its claims and promises beyond the immediate recipient."[10] This captures the movement that defines this section. The covenant reaches forward, carrying the purpose of God through time.

Continuing movement

As this chapter comes to a close, the movement that began with Abraham's calling becomes clearer. The covenant has provided structure. The promise has gained stability. Responsibility has shaped participation. Election has defined purpose. Identity has taken form. Now, continuity ensures that the journey does not end.

The story moves from one life to a people. What began with Abraham now prepares the way for a community that will carry this purpose into the future. The covenant becomes the framework through which this movement continues.

This progression holds everything together. It shows that God's work does not fade with time. It grows, extends, and continues. The journey that began with a single step now moves forward through generations, shaping a people who will live within this covenant and carry its purpose into the world.

---

[10] Gordon J. Wenham, "The Theology of the Book of Genesis," *Journal for the Study of the Old Testament* 34, no. 1 (2009): 16.

CHAPTER 3 — EXODUS AND REDEMPTIVE IDENTITY

The narrative of covenant promise enters a decisive historical turning point when identity is no longer shaped in anticipation, but within the pressure of oppression and deliverance. In Egypt, the descendants of Abraham move from remembered promise into lived affliction, where the language of suffering becomes the setting for divine intervention. Redemption does not appear as abstraction or distant assurance, but as a disruptive act within history that redefines how the people understand both God and themselves. What was once a family shaped by promise now becomes a community formed through liberation.

This chapter traces how deliverance becomes the foundation of identity, not only by removing oppression but by creating memory that binds the people together. The journey out of Egypt, through wilderness formation, and toward emerging communal consciousness reveals that redemption is not an endpoint but a beginning of collective formation. In this movement, identity is no longer primarily inherited through ancestry or expectation, but shaped through shared experience of divine action in history.

Deliverance from Bondage

The story now enters a space where promise meets pain. The descendants of Abraham are no longer walking as a family guided by direction and covenant. They are living under pressure, their days shaped by forced labor, their lives measured by the demands of a system that sees them only as workers. The Bible describes this condition with stark clarity: "They made their lives bitter with hard service" (Exodus 1:14). What began as a place of provision in Egypt has turned into a place of confinement. The people who carried a promise now carry burdens.

Under oppression

The reality of slavery in Egypt is not presented as a distant background detail. It fills the scene. Families wake up each day to the same unending labor. Strength is spent on tasks that offer no dignity. The rhythm of life becomes controlled by another power. In Exodus 1:13–14, the language reflects intensity and weight, as if every moment presses down on them. Their identity begins to shrink under the force of oppression.

This kind of experience has echoed in many parts of the world. In a rural brick kiln in South Asia, entire families have worked for years under debt that never reduces. Generation after generation carries the same burden, shaping how they see themselves and their future. Their story reflects something similar to what Israel faced in Egypt. Bondage does more than control the body. It slowly shapes the mind and the sense of identity.

A cry that rises

Within this heavy condition, something begins to move. The people cry out. The Bible says, "The people of Israel groaned because of their slavery and cried out for help" (Exodus 2:23). This cry is not organized. It is not polished. It rises from pain, from exhaustion, from longing for change. It is the sound of people who reach the limit of their strength.

What follows is one of the most significant movements in the narrative. "God heard their groaning, and God remembered his covenant with Abraham, with Isaac, and with Jacob" (Exodus 2:24). The covenant that shaped earlier generations now becomes active within this moment. God sees. God hears. God knows. The suffering of the people does not remain hidden. It enters the awareness of God in a way that leads to action.

There are moments in human life when prayer takes this same form. In a hospital ward filled with uncertainty, a father once sat beside his child, unable to speak long sentences. His prayer came in short, broken words. Yet those words carried everything within them. In a similar way, the cry of Israel carries their whole reality before God.

A messenger called

God's response begins quietly, away from the noise of Egypt. Moses is in the wilderness when he encounters the burning bush. In Exodus 3:7–8, God speaks directly: "I have surely seen the affliction of my people… and I have come down to deliver them." These words connect divine awareness with divine action. God does not remain distant. He steps into the situation.

Moses becomes part of this movement. He is called to stand between God and the people, between God and Pharaoh. His calling does not arise from his own ambition. It comes from God's initiative. At first, Moses hesitates. He questions his ability and his role. Yet the focus remains clear. God's presence will go with him. "I will be with you" (Exodus 3:12) becomes the assurance that carries him forward.

This pattern continues in many stories of service. A young teacher once left a secure career to work among migrant children who had no access to education. She carried uncertainty and questions, yet she stepped forward because she sensed a deeper calling. Over time, her presence became a channel through which change began. In a similar way, Moses becomes the one through whom God begins to act within history.

Power revealed

As Moses returns to Egypt, the confrontation begins. The plagues are not random events. They unfold as a series of acts that reveal God's authority. Each moment challenges the power structures of Egypt. In Exodus 7:5, the purpose becomes clear: "The Egyptians shall know that I am the Lord."

The Nile turns to blood. Darkness covers the land. The patterns of life are disrupted. These events speak beyond Israel. They make visible the reality that God is present and active. Pharaoh resists, hardening his heart again and again. Yet the movement continues. Each act pushes the story closer to its turning point.

These moments show that redemption involves confrontation. It addresses forces that hold people in bondage. It brings to light what has remained unchallenged. In various parts of the world, movements against injustice have often followed this pattern. Truth becomes visible, systems are questioned, and change begins to take shape.

A decisive release

The final movement comes with the Passover. In Exodus 12, a clear instruction is given. A lamb is prepared. Its blood marks the doors. The act is simple, yet it carries deep meaning. It becomes the sign of protection and transition.

That night changes everything. The power that held the people begins to break. Pharaoh releases them. "And the

Egyptians urged the people to hurry and leave the land" (Exodus 12:33). What seemed impossible now takes place. The people who lived under forced labor begin to move toward freedom.

This release is not gradual. It is decisive. It marks a clear turning point. The people step out of Egypt carrying more than their belongings. They carry a new understanding of God and of themselves. They begin to see that their story is shaped by divine action.

Beginning of identity

Deliverance becomes the starting point of a new identity. The people are no longer defined by slavery. They are defined by what God has done for them. In Exodus 13:3, Moses reminds them, "Remember this day in which you came out from Egypt, out of the house of slavery, for by a strong hand the Lord brought you out."

This moment stays with them. It becomes the reference point for how they understand their past and their future. Redemption shapes their memory, their language, and their direction.

As one scholar observes, "The exodus is the central saving act of God in the Old Testament, forming the identity of Israel as a redeemed people."[11] This insight captures the weight of what has taken place. Deliverance does more than remove suffering. It creates a people who now live with a clear sense of who they are.

The movement from bondage to freedom now stands at the center of their story. It prepares the way for everything that follows. The covenant that was spoken now becomes lived. The people who cried out now walk forward. Their journey has begun, and their identity has been formed through the powerful act of redemption.

Formation of Collective Identity

The night of departure did more than open a path out of Egypt. It gathered a people into a shared story. What had existed as many families, each carrying its own struggles and memories, now began to move as one body. The Bible describes this movement with quiet force: "The people of Israel journeyed…

---

[11] Brevard S. Childs, "The Book of Exodus: A Critical, Theological Commentary," *Journal of Biblical Literature* 95, no. 3 (1976): 358.

about six hundred thousand men on foot, besides women and children" (Exodus 12:37). This is more than a count. It is the first glimpse of a community emerging from scattered households into a united people. They walk together, and in that walking, something new begins to take shape.

From families to a people

Before this moment, identity rested in smaller circles. Each family knew its own history, its own hardships, its own way of surviving under oppression. Now, the experience of deliverance gathers them into a larger belonging. They no longer move as isolated groups. They move with a shared direction. The road itself becomes a place where identity shifts.

The Bible gives a simple yet powerful detail: "A mixed multitude also went up with them" (Exodus 12:38). The community is not uniform. It carries diversity within it. Yet they are drawn together by a common event. Redemption becomes the thread that holds them. What defines them is no longer where they came from, but what they have experienced together.

In one coastal region of Southeast Asia, after a devastating cyclone, entire villages were displaced. Families who had never interacted closely began living side by side in temporary shelters. Over time, something changed. They shared food, rebuilt homes together, and told their stories to one another. Their identity slowly shifted from isolated households to a community shaped by shared survival. In a deeper way, Israel begins to experience this kind of transformation as they move out of Egypt.

Identity through shared deliverance

As the journey continues, the memory of what God has done becomes central. The people begin to speak of themselves in a new way. They are the ones whom God brought out. This shared experience creates a bond that goes beyond bloodlines.

Moses repeatedly reminds them of this reality. "You shall remember that you were a slave in the land of Egypt, and the Lord your God brought you out" (Deuteronomy 5:15). This remembrance is not meant to keep them in the past. It shapes how they see themselves in the present. Their identity is rooted in an act of deliverance that all of them share.

This kind of identity carries strength. It forms unity that does not depend on status or background. Each person stands on equal ground within the story. Every family has walked through the same moment of release. Every voice can say, "We were brought out."

The journey as formation

The path from Egypt does not immediately lead to a settled place. It leads into the wilderness. At first glance, the wilderness appears uncertain and empty. Yet it becomes a space where identity deepens.

In Exodus 13:21, the Bible describes how the Lord goes before them "by day in a pillar of cloud… and by night in a pillar of fire." This constant presence shapes how the people understand their relationship with God. They are not simply a group that escaped oppression. They are a people being led.

The journey teaches them to depend on this guidance. When they face hunger, provision comes. When they face thirst, water is given. Each moment forms their understanding of who God is and who they are in relation to Him. Identity grows through these experiences, not through abstract ideas but through daily encounters.

A field worker in Central Asia once described how a small group of new believers learned to trust God while traveling between remote villages. They had little certainty about where they would stay or how they would be received. Yet each day brought unexpected provision. Over time, their identity was shaped by this journey. They began to see themselves as a people carried by God's presence. In a similar way, Israel's journey becomes the ground where their identity takes root.

Relationship shaped by God's action

The defining feature of this emerging identity lies in relationship. The people begin to understand that they belong to God because of what He has done. In Exodus 6:7, God declares, "I will take you to be my people, and I will be your God." This statement gives direction to everything that follows.

Belonging is no longer tied to location or condition. It is tied to relationship. The people carry this awareness as they move forward. They are not simply free individuals. They are a people connected to God through a shared experience of deliverance.

This relationship shapes how they see one another. It creates a sense of mutual belonging. Each person stands within the same covenantal reality. Each life is part of a larger whole. The story they carry becomes the foundation of their unity.

A people belonging to God

As the journey unfolds, the language of belonging becomes clearer. The people are described as God's own possession, a people set apart through His action. In Exodus 19:4–5, God reminds them, "You yourselves have seen what I did… and how I bore you on eagles' wings and brought you to myself."

This image captures the heart of their identity. They have been carried. They have been brought into relationship. Their existence as a people is rooted in this movement. They belong to God, and that belonging shapes every aspect of their life.

One scholar reflects on this transformation by stating, "Israel's identity is grounded in the shared memory of deliverance, which becomes the defining marker of the community's self-understanding."[12] This insight highlights how deeply redemption shapes who they are.

The movement from scattered families to a unified people now stands complete. Identity has begun to form through shared experience, ongoing journey, and relationship with God. The people who once lived under oppression now carry a new understanding of themselves. They walk forward as a community shaped by redemption, prepared for the next stage of their calling.

Divine Power and Public Display

The story of deliverance never remains hidden. What began as a cry in the night becomes a series of events that the whole land of Egypt cannot ignore. God's action does not unfold in a quiet corner. It takes place in the center of power, before rulers, officials, and ordinary people. The redemption of Israel becomes visible. It carries a weight that forces attention. The Bible presents this clearly when God says, "The Egyptians shall know that I am the Lord" (Exodus 7:5). What happens in Egypt reveals who God is.

Power revealed through the plagues

The plagues come one after another, each one striking at the heart of Egyptian life. Water turns to blood. Darkness covers

---

[12] Frank Crüsemann, "The Theology of the Exodus Tradition," *Interpretation* 38, no. 1 (1984): 19.

the land. Crops fail. Livestock perish. These are not random disasters. They move with purpose. Each moment speaks against the powers that hold the people in bondage.

Pharaoh stands as the visible symbol of authority, yet with every plague his power weakens. His words lose their force. His control begins to slip. The narrative shows a steady unveiling of a greater authority. God's power does not appear as a distant idea. It is experienced in ways that affect the entire land.

The people of Israel witness this unfolding. They begin to understand that their deliverance is not achieved through their strength. It comes through the decisive action of God. Their identity as a redeemed people grows deeper as they see what God is able to do.

Confrontation with structures of power

The plagues do more than demonstrate power. They confront a system that has defined itself as unchallenged. Egypt represents a structured world where authority flows from the top and extends into every part of life. Slavery is sustained by this structure.

Through each act, God disrupts this system. The Nile, which supports life, becomes undrinkable. The sky, which brings light, becomes dark. The ground, which produces food, fails to yield. The familiar patterns that sustain Egypt begin to collapse.

This confrontation shows that redemption involves more than removing people from hardship. It addresses the structures that create and maintain that hardship. The people of Israel see that the God who calls them also stands against forces that limit and control life.

In a modern setting, there was a time when workers in a large industrial zone lived under harsh conditions with little voice. A small group began to raise concerns, bringing attention to practices that had long remained hidden. As their voices grew, the system itself began to change. What seemed fixed started to shift. In a deeper and more powerful way, the events in Egypt reveal that God steps into history to confront what holds people in bondage.

God's name made known

As the events unfold, one theme becomes clear. God is making Himself known. This knowledge does not come through explanation alone. It comes through action. Each plague carries a message. Each moment reveals something about who God is.

When Moses stands before Pharaoh, the words he speaks carry this purpose. "Thus says the Lord" becomes the repeated phrase that frames every encounter. God's name is spoken, and then it is demonstrated. The connection between word and action becomes visible.

For the people of Israel, this revelation shapes their understanding of God. He is not distant. He is present. He acts within their history. He reveals Himself in ways that they can see and remember. Their faith begins to take form around what they have witnessed.

Redemption seen by others

The events in Egypt reach beyond the boundaries of Israel. The surrounding people cannot ignore what is happening. News travels. Stories spread. The power displayed in Egypt becomes known in other places.

Later in the narrative, when the people approach new lands, there are those who already recognize what has happened. In Joshua 2:10, Rahab speaks of what she has heard: "We have heard how the Lord dried up the water of the Red Sea before you." The memory of God's action in Egypt moves beyond Israel and shapes how others respond.

This shows that redemption carries a public dimension. It is not only for those who experience it directly. It becomes a witness. It reveals something about God to the wider world. The people of Israel carry a story that others come to know.

Recognition beyond Israel

As the plagues reach their final stage, the distinction between Israel and Egypt becomes clear. The land of Goshen, where the Israelites live, remains protected while the rest of Egypt experiences the full force of the events. This distinction highlights the relationship between God and His people.

At the same time, there are Egyptians who begin to respond differently. Some heed the warnings given through Moses. Some acknowledge the power they are witnessing. The narrative leaves space for recognition that extends beyond a single group.

In Exodus 12:38, the mention of a "mixed multitude" leaving Egypt suggests that others join the movement. They see what God has done, and they respond. Redemption begins to draw people beyond its original boundaries.

A scholar reflects on this dimension by noting, "The plagues function as a revelation of divine sovereignty, not only to Israel but to Egypt and the wider world."[13] This captures the way these events move outward, making God known in a broader context.

Power that shapes identity

For Israel, these events become foundational. They have seen God act in ways that cannot be forgotten. This shapes their understanding of who they are. They are a people delivered by a powerful God, a God who reveals Himself openly and decisively.

This awareness stays with them as they continue their journey. When they face new challenges, they remember what they have seen. The power displayed in Egypt becomes a source of confidence and direction.

The story of redemption now carries both personal and public meaning. It shapes the identity of the people, and it reveals God to the world. The movement continues, leading from visible power toward a deeper understanding of purpose.

Redemption and Purpose

The people have crossed out of Egypt. The weight of slavery has lifted. The night of fear has given way to a morning of movement. Yet the story does not pause at freedom. It continues forward with direction. The Bible presents this shift with quiet clarity. God speaks to Moses and says, "When you have brought the people out of Egypt, you shall serve God on this mountain" (Exodus 3:12). Freedom opens a path, and that path leads somewhere. It carries purpose.

Freedom as a beginning

The first steps into the wilderness feel like release. The people sing, they rejoice, they remember what has just happened. In Exodus 15, the song of Moses rises as a response to deliverance. Yet even within this celebration, there is movement.

---

[13] Terence E. Fretheim, "The Plagues as Ecological Signs of Judgment," *Interpretation* 37, no. 4 (1983): 386.

The journey continues. Freedom becomes the starting point of something new.

The Bible does not present liberation as a final destination. It presents it as an entry into a different kind of life. The people are no longer under Pharaoh, yet they are being led toward a deeper relationship with God. This shift begins to reshape how freedom is understood. It is not only about leaving something behind. It is about stepping into something ahead.

In one region of East Africa, a group of families once lived under constant conflict, moving from place to place for safety. When peace was established, they finally settled in one location. At first, they celebrated the end of danger. Over time, they began to ask a different question: What kind of life do we build now? Their freedom created space for purpose. In a similar way, Israel's deliverance begins to open a future that must be lived with direction.

Toward Sinai

The movement of the people leads them to a mountain. The wilderness, which seemed empty, now becomes a pathway. In Exodus 19:4–5, God speaks again: "I bore you on eagles' wings and brought you to myself… you shall be my treasured possession among all peoples." The journey is revealed as intentional. The people have been brought out in order to be brought near.

Sinai becomes a place where identity and purpose begin to take clearer form. The God who delivered them now draws them into relationship. The movement from Egypt to Sinai is not random travel. It is a guided transition from rescue to belonging.

This moment shows that redemption carries direction. It leads into a space where life is shaped, where purpose is revealed, and where the people begin to understand their role within a larger plan.

Purpose shaping freedom

As the people move forward, their understanding of freedom deepens. It is no longer defined by the absence of oppression alone. It begins to be shaped by how they live. The question shifts from "What have we escaped?" to "How do we now live?"

In Exodus 19:6, God describes them as "a kingdom of priests and a holy nation." This statement gives form to their purpose. Their freedom is meant to reflect something greater. It carries a responsibility that shapes their daily life, their relationships, and their direction.

Freedom without purpose can drift. It can return to patterns that once held it captive. Yet when purpose enters, freedom gains direction. It becomes a space where life aligns with intention. The people begin to see that their lives are meant to reflect the God who has delivered them.

A small community in Central Asia once received access to education after generations of limitation. At first, the focus rested on opportunity. Over time, leaders within the community began to guide the younger generation toward using that education to serve others, to build schools, and to create spaces for growth. Their freedom gained purpose. It moved beyond personal benefit into shared responsibility. In a deeper way, Israel begins to understand that their freedom is meant to carry meaning beyond themselves.

Representing God among the nations

The purpose given to Israel extends outward. They are called to represent God in the midst of the world. Their identity is not isolated. It carries a wider horizon. The language of being a "kingdom of priests" suggests a role that connects God and humanity.

This calling shapes how they are to live. Their actions, their values, and their relationships become a reflection of the God they belong to. The nations around them will see something through them. Their story will speak beyond their own experience.

This idea does not emerge as a distant concept. It begins to take root in how they walk, how they respond, and how they remember. Their journey itself becomes a witness. The God who delivered them is made known through their life as a people.

Alignment with divine intention

As the chapter moves forward, one theme becomes clear. Redemption brings alignment. The people who once lived under another authority now learn to live under God's direction. This alignment touches every part of life. It shapes choices, relationships, and priorities.

In Exodus 15:13, the song of Moses includes these words: "You have led in your steadfast love the people whom you have redeemed; you have guided them by your strength to your holy abode." The language of leading and guiding reflects ongoing movement. Redemption does not end with a single event. It continues as a journey shaped by God's presence.

This alignment does not remove challenges. The wilderness brings moments of testing and uncertainty. Yet within these moments, the people are invited to trust and to follow. Their freedom becomes the space where this trust is lived out.

A scholar captures this movement with clarity: "The exodus is not simply deliverance from something but deliverance for something, a new life under the rule and purpose of God."[14] This insight holds together the heart of the narrative. Redemption opens a future, and that future carries direction.

The people now stand between what they have left and what lies ahead. Their identity has been shaped through deliverance. Their path now leads into purpose. The journey continues, carrying them toward a deeper understanding of who they are and why they have been brought out.

Memory and Continuity

The journey out of Egypt does not fade into silence once the people begin to move forward. It settles into their memory, shaping how they understand every step that follows. What God has done becomes too weighty to be left behind. It must be carried, spoken, and remembered. The Bible gives this responsibility a clear form when God says, "This day shall be for you a memorial day, and you shall keep it as a feast to the Lord" (Exodus 12:14). Redemption becomes something to remember, not only as history, but as a living reality that continues to shape the people.

Remembering through Passover

The Passover stands at the center of this remembrance. It is not merely an event that happened once. It becomes a practice that returns again and again. Each year, the people gather, prepare the meal, and retell the story. The lamb, the bread, the night of deliverance all come back into the present through this act.

---

[14] Rolf Rendtorff, "The Significance of the Exodus Tradition," *Journal for the Study of the Old Testament* 14, no. 27 (1983): 22.

The Bible places this responsibility within the life of the family. "When your children say to you, 'What do you mean by this service?' you shall say, 'It is the sacrifice of the Lord's Passover'" (Exodus 12:26–27). The question of a child becomes the doorway for the story to be spoken again. Memory is not left to chance. It is intentionally passed on.

In one mountain village in Nepal, a small community gathers each year to remember the day their village was rebuilt after a landslide. Elders sit with the younger ones and tell the story in detail. They speak of loss, of help that came from unexpected places, and of how the village stood again. The children grow up knowing this story as part of who they are. In a deeper way, Israel carries its story of deliverance through the practice of Passover.

Story carried across generations

The power of memory lies in its ability to travel. The people who stood on the night of deliverance will not always be there to tell it. Yet the story continues. It moves from one generation to the next, carried through words, actions, and shared practices.

In Exodus 13:8, the instruction is clear: "You shall tell your son on that day, 'It is because of what the Lord did for me when I came out of Egypt.'" The language is personal. Each generation speaks as though they themselves were part of the event. The past becomes present through remembrance.

This way of remembering creates continuity. It ensures that identity does not weaken over time. The people remain connected to the same moment of redemption, even as years pass. The story becomes the thread that holds them together across generations.

Memory shaping identity

As the story is retold, it begins to shape how the people see themselves. They understand who they are through what God has done. Their identity remains rooted in deliverance. They are a people who were brought out, a people who were carried through the night into freedom.

This memory influences how they respond to life. It shapes their trust in God. It guides their decisions. It reminds them that their existence as a people is tied to an act of grace and power.

In Deuteronomy 6:20–21, this connection becomes even clearer: "When your son asks you in time to come… then you shall say… 'We were Pharaoh's slaves in Egypt. And the Lord brought us out of Egypt with a mighty hand.'" The answer to the question of identity begins with remembrance.

In many communities shaped by hardship and renewal, memory carries this same role. In parts of Latin America, groups that experienced conflict have preserved their stories through songs and gatherings. These memories guide how they live and how they relate to one another. In Israel's story, remembrance serves a similar purpose, grounding identity in a shared experience of redemption.

Repetition and retelling

Memory grows stronger through repetition. The story is told again and again, not as a routine, but as a way of keeping the reality alive. Each telling brings the past into the present. Each gathering renews the awareness of what God has done.

This repetition creates stability. It protects the people from forgetting. It anchors them in a truth that remains constant even when circumstances change. The wilderness journey, the challenges ahead, and the future they will enter all find their meaning in this remembered event.

The rhythm of remembering becomes part of their life. It shapes their calendar, their gatherings, and their conversations. The story of deliverance becomes the foundation upon which everything else stands.

Future grounded in redemption

As the people look ahead, their memory guides them. The past becomes the lens through which they see the future. They move forward with the confidence that the God who acted before continues to lead them.

This connection between past and future gives direction to their journey. It reminds them that they are part of a story that continues. The same God who brought them out will guide them into what lies ahead.

A scholar reflects on this dynamic by stating, "Israel's rituals of remembrance serve to actualize the past, allowing each generation to participate in the foundational event of redemption."[15] This insight captures the living nature of memory within the community.

The chapter now reaches its natural conclusion. Deliverance has taken place. A people has been formed. Power has been revealed. Purpose has been given. Memory now holds everything together. It carries the story forward, ensuring that what began in Egypt continues to shape every generation that follows.

The people walk on, holding their past close, stepping into their future with a clear sense of who they are.

[15] Baruch J. Schwartz, "Memory and Identity in the Exodus Tradition," *Journal of Biblical Literature* 127, no. 1 (2008): 47.

CHAPTER 4 — KINGDOM OF PRIESTS AND LAW

The movement from redemption into formation reaches a decisive moment at Sinai, where identity begins to take structured expression through instruction and communal order. What was experienced as deliverance in Egypt now becomes a defined way of life in the wilderness, where a people are not only freed from oppression but shaped for representation. At this point in the narrative, belonging is no longer simply remembered through past rescue, but expressed through a present calling that gives direction to daily life.

Within this setting, law emerges not as limitation but as formation, shaping a community that reflects divine character in visible and structured ways. The designation of Israel as a kingdom of priests introduces a vocation that extends beyond internal cohesion toward outward representation within the world. This chapter follows how identity is formed through instruction, how community life is ordered through divine guidance, and how vocation begins to define the people not only in relation to themselves, but in relation to the wider human context.

Priestly Identity

The people stand at the foot of the mountain. The journey from Egypt has brought them here, to a place where the air feels different, where expectation gathers like a quiet weight. They have seen deliverance. They have walked through the wilderness. Now they begin to hear words that define who they are becoming. The Bible records this moment with striking clarity: "You shall be to me a kingdom of priests and a holy nation" (Exodus 19:6). These words do more than describe. They call the people into a new way of understanding themselves.

Declaration at Sinai

This declaration comes before the law is fully given. It comes before detailed instructions shape their daily life. Identity is spoken first. The people hear who they are meant to be even before they learn how to live it out. Sinai becomes the place where purpose is named.

The mountain itself becomes a meeting point. God draws near, and the people gather at a distance, aware that something significant is unfolding. Moses moves between God and the people, carrying words that shape their future. The statement "kingdom of priests" rises in this setting, giving direction to everything that follows.

The people who once lived under the authority of Egypt now hear a different voice. Their identity is no longer defined by what they escaped. It begins to be defined by what they are called to become.

Identity rooted in relationship

This identity grows out of relationship. Just before this declaration, God reminds them, "You yourselves have seen what I did… and how I bore you on eagles' wings and brought you to myself" (Exodus 19:4). The foundation is clear. They belong to God because He has brought them near.

Being a "kingdom of priests" begins with belonging. It is not a role taken up through effort. It is a response to a relationship already given. The people are invited to live out what they have received. Their identity flows from being known and called by God.

In one rural region of South India, a teacher gathered children each evening under a large tree. Many of them came from difficult homes, carrying burdens beyond their age. The teacher did not begin with lessons. She began by telling them, "You matter. You belong here." Over time, the children started to change. Their actions, their confidence, and their relationships reflected the truth they had received. In a deeper way, Israel begins to live from the identity spoken to them at Sinai.

Mediation between God and the nations

The idea of priesthood carries meaning that reaches beyond ritual. A priest stands in a place of connection. A priest represents God to people and brings people toward God. When the whole nation is called a kingdom of priests, this role expands to include everyone.

The people are positioned within the world with a purpose that extends outward. Their life together becomes a space where

God is made known. They are not gathered only for their own sake. They stand as a community through which others may begin to see and understand God.

This calling does not remove them from the world. It places them within it with a clear role. Their presence among the nations carries meaning. Their story, their practices, and their relationships become ways through which God's character is revealed.

Representation through life

Representation takes shape in daily living. It is seen in how the people relate to one another, how they respond to challenges, and how they carry themselves in the world. The identity of priesthood is not confined to specific moments. It touches every part of life.

As the people move forward from Sinai, their actions begin to reflect this calling. Their life becomes a visible expression of their relationship with God. The way they treat one another, the way they honor God, and the way they engage with others all become part of this representation.

A small community in Central Asia once became known for the way its members cared for one another during a season of hardship. Outsiders who observed them began to ask questions. What gave them such unity? What shaped their actions? Without formal speeches or structured teaching, their life itself became a testimony. In a similar way, Israel's calling as a priestly people begins to take form through how they live.

A shared vocation

This identity belongs to the whole community. It is not limited to a select group. Every person stands within this calling. The language of "kingdom" points to a collective reality. The people together carry this role.

This shared vocation creates a sense of unity. Each individual life contributes to a larger purpose. No one stands outside the calling. Each person's actions, choices, and relationships become part of the community's witness.

The people begin to see themselves not only as individuals or families, but as a people with a shared purpose. Their identity binds them together, shaping how they move forward as one body.

A scholar captures this idea with clarity: "Israel's priestly identity expresses a corporate vocation, in which the whole people are called to mediate the knowledge of God to the nations."[16] This insight reflects the depth of what is spoken at Sinai.

The section comes to rest with a clear sense of direction. The people who were delivered now receive a calling that defines their place in the world. Their identity is rooted in relationship, expressed through life, and shared across the community. The journey continues, moving from identity into formation, where this calling will begin to take shape in every aspect of their life.

Law as Formation

The voice from the mountain does not fade after identity is spoken. It continues, shaping how the people are to live in the world they are entering. At Sinai, words are given that touch every part of life. They are not distant instructions meant for occasional reference. They are words meant to shape movement, relationships, decisions, and worship. The Bible describes this moment as God speaking to His people so that they may walk in His ways (Exodus 20:1–2). What follows is not only command, but formation.

Law as instruction for living

The law begins with clarity. It speaks into the ordinary patterns of life. How people treat one another, how justice is practiced, how worship is expressed, and how rest is honored all come into view. These instructions are not detached from life. They enter into it.

In the ancient world around Israel, many communities lived under shifting systems of rule. Laws often reflected the power of rulers rather than the well being of people. In contrast, what emerges at Sinai presents a different direction. The law is spoken within relationship. It begins with the reminder that God has brought the people out of Egypt. The instruction flows from redemption.

The people begin to understand that their daily life is now shaped by a different voice. The law becomes a guide that reaches

---

[16] John J. Collins, "A Kingdom of Priests: The Role of Israel in Exodus 19:6," *Journal of Biblical Literature* 135, no. 2 (2016): 289.

into ordinary actions, giving direction where confusion once existed.

Formation of habits and patterns

As the instructions are received, they begin to shape rhythm. Life takes on patterns that reflect the presence of God. Rest becomes part of time. Justice becomes part of community life. Honesty becomes part of speech and trade.

These patterns are not formed in a single moment. They grow through repetition. The people begin to learn what it means to live in a way that reflects what they have received. The law slowly becomes part of their identity through practice.

In a coastal village in East Africa, fishermen once adjusted their way of working after new shared agreements were introduced to preserve the sea's resources. At first, it felt unfamiliar. Over time, the rhythm of their work changed. Their habits began to reflect a new understanding of responsibility toward creation and community. In a deeper sense, Israel begins to form habits that reflect their relationship with God.

Integration of worship and daily life

At Sinai, worship is not separated from life. The same God who gives instruction for daily relationships also shapes how He is worshiped. Sacrifice, rest, and remembrance are woven into the life of the people.

This integration creates unity. There is no division between sacred moments and ordinary moments. The presence of God is acknowledged in both. Life itself becomes a space where worship is expressed.

When the people later set up their camps, their structure reflects this understanding. The center of their community becomes a place of meeting with God. Around it, life unfolds in ordered relationship. Worship and life remain connected, forming a continuous expression of belonging.

Guidance for relationships

The law speaks directly into human relationships. It addresses honesty, respect, care, and justice. It shapes how people treat neighbors, strangers, and family members. These instructions begin to form a community where life together reflects divine intention.

This guidance creates boundaries that protect life and relationships. It also creates space for trust. The people learn that living together requires attention, responsibility, and care. The law becomes a framework that holds community life in balance.

In one urban neighborhood in South Asia, a group of residents began to rebuild trust after years of division. Simple agreements about shared spaces, mutual respect, and cooperation gradually changed how people interacted. Over time, relationships began to heal. In a similar way, the law given at Sinai begins to reshape how Israel lives together.

Law as gift rather than burden

As the people receive these instructions, they begin to discover something deeper. The law is not presented as a weight placed upon them. It is given as a gift that shapes life. It provides direction where confusion once existed. It offers clarity where uncertainty once ruled.

This understanding grows over time. The people begin to see that the law is part of their relationship with God. It reflects His character and invites them into a way of life that mirrors that character.

In Psalm 19, later reflection captures this sense: "The law of the Lord is perfect, reviving the soul." The law is seen as life giving, not restricting. It becomes a source of stability and guidance for a people learning how to live in freedom.

A scholar observes, "Torah in the Sinai tradition functions as formative instruction, shaping Israel into a covenant community through lived practice rather than abstract regulation."[17] This insight reflects the lived reality of what is happening among the people.

The section comes to a natural pause. The people who received identity at Sinai now receive direction for life. Their actions, relationships, and worship begin to take shape through the words spoken to them. The journey continues into a deeper understanding of what it means to live as a people formed by God.

---

[17] Gordon J. Wenham, "The Theology of Torah in Exodus," *Tyndale Bulletin* 41, no. 2 (1990): 203.

Holiness and Distinction

The people who stand at Sinai are not only given identity and instruction. They are also given a direction for how that identity is to be expressed in the world around them. The word that begins to shape this life is holiness. It enters their story as a call to live in a way that reflects the One who has called them. "You shall be holy, for I am holy" (Leviticus 11:44) becomes a steady reminder that their life is meant to mirror God's character in visible ways.

Holiness as relational reality

Holiness begins with relationship. It is not first about distance or separation. It is about belonging to God. The people are set apart because they are known and claimed by Him. This belonging gives meaning to every part of their life.

At Sinai, holiness is introduced within the context of presence. God is not distant from His people. He is among them. The cloud, the voice, and the covenant all point to a relationship that is alive and active. From this relationship, a way of living begins to take shape.

In a quiet farming region of South India, a small group of families once began to reorganize their shared life after experiencing renewal in their community. The change did not begin with rules. It began with a sense of belonging to something deeper than themselves. Their daily decisions slowly began to reflect that new awareness. In a similar way, Israel begins to understand holiness as life shaped by relationship.

Distinction without isolation

Being set apart does not mean being removed from the world. The people are called to live among others while carrying a distinct identity. Their distinction is meant to be visible, not hidden. It shapes how they live, how they speak, and how they respond to the world around them.

This distinction creates clarity. It allows the people to live with a sense of direction that is not dependent on surrounding cultures. Yet it does not close them off. Their presence among the nations remains important. They are placed within history as a people who carry a different way of life.

In a historic port city along the Mediterranean, small trading communities once maintained distinct cultural practices while engaging daily with people from many nations. Their identity remained visible through their habits, their gatherings, and their values. They were not isolated, yet they remained distinct. Israel's calling begins to reflect a similar pattern within a deeper spiritual frame.

Reflecting divine character

Holiness becomes visible through reflection. The life of the people is meant to reflect the character of God. This includes justice, mercy, faithfulness, and truth. These qualities begin to shape how the community lives together and how they respond to others.

The instructions given at Sinai are not only about behavior. They point toward character formation. The people begin to learn what it means for their actions to reflect the One who has brought them out of Egypt. Their life becomes a living testimony of His presence among them.

Over time, this reflection shapes how others see them. The way they treat one another becomes part of their witness. Their shared life begins to reveal something beyond themselves.

Boundaries shaping identity

Holiness also involves boundaries. These boundaries are not meant to limit life but to protect it. They create space for identity to remain clear and focused. The instructions given at Sinai establish patterns that guide how the people are to live within their covenant relationship.

These boundaries help the people understand who they are and who they are not. They provide structure that supports their calling. Within these boundaries, life becomes ordered and meaningful.

In a pastoral region of East Africa, communities once established shared agreements about land use to protect both people and environment. These boundaries did not restrict life. They preserved it. They allowed communities to flourish without losing identity or balance. In a deeper sense, Israel's boundaries shape a life that remains centered on God's presence.

Presence of God defining life

At the heart of holiness is presence. The defining feature of Israel's life is that God is with them. The tabernacle that will later be built becomes a visible reminder of this truth. God does not remain distant. He dwells among His people.

This presence reshapes everything. It gives meaning to their actions, direction to their journey, and purpose to their community life. Holiness becomes a response to this presence. It is life lived in awareness of God who is near.

A scholar observes, "Holiness in the Sinai tradition functions as a relational identity formed through the presence of God among the community, shaping ethical and social life."[18] This insight reflects the way holiness begins to take shape within Israel's story.

The section settles with clarity. The people who were delivered and formed now begin to live in a way that reflects distinction. Their life is shaped by relationship, guided by boundaries, and marked by presence. Holiness becomes the visible expression of who they are becoming as a people.

Social Structure and Order

The people who have received identity, instruction, and a call to holiness now begin to face a deeper question. How should a community shaped by God actually live together in daily life? At Sinai, the answer begins to take form through laws that touch relationships, justice, responsibility, and care. The vision is not abstract. It is practical. It reaches into how people treat one another in ordinary situations, shaping a society that reflects divine intention in visible ways.

Justice within community

Justice becomes one of the clearest expressions of life under God's instruction. It is not presented as an ideal placed at a distance. It enters courts, disputes, agreements, and daily interactions. The people are taught that fairness is part of their covenant life.

In Exodus 23, instructions emphasize careful judgment and honesty in dealing with others. Justice is to be free from distortion, whether by influence, fear, or advantage. This creates a foundation where truth is valued within the community.

---

[18] Jacob Milgrom, "The Dynamics of Holiness in Ancient Israel," *Harvard Theological Review* 94, no. 2 (2001): 145.

In a growing settlement in Southeast Asia, village leaders once introduced shared practices for resolving disputes through collective discussion rather than private influence. Over time, trust began to grow among families who had previously been divided. Justice, when practiced with consistency, began to reshape relationships. In a similar way, Israel's community life begins to reflect justice as part of its covenant identity.

Care for vulnerable members

The law also gives attention to those who are most vulnerable. The stranger, the widow, and the orphan are repeatedly mentioned within the instructions. Their presence in the community is not overlooked. It is intentionally protected.

This care reflects the character of God who delivered the people from oppression. Having experienced deliverance themselves, they are now instructed to extend care to others who may be in need. Memory becomes action. What they received becomes what they are called to give.

In a coastal region of East Africa, fishing communities once developed shared systems to support families during seasons of low catch. Resources were shared so that no household was left without support. This practice grew not from abundance alone but from shared understanding of vulnerability. Israel's instruction begins to shape a similar awareness within covenant life.

Order in social relationships

Order within the community is not about control. It is about stability. The law provides structure for how people relate to one another in family life, work, and community interaction. These patterns create clarity and reduce confusion in relationships.

The instructions given at Sinai include guidance on honesty in speech, fairness in trade, and respect within family relationships. These elements combine to form a society where life can be lived with trust. Order becomes a foundation for healthy community life.

In a developing urban neighborhood in South Asia, residents once agreed on simple shared practices for maintaining common spaces. Over time, these practices reduced tension and increased cooperation. Order in daily life allowed relationships to grow stronger. In a deeper sense, Israel begins to experience order as part of covenant living.

Balance between authority and responsibility

Within the structure of the community, authority is present, but it is not isolated from responsibility. Leaders are given guidance on how to act with fairness and care. Authority is shaped by accountability to God and responsibility toward people.

This balance ensures that leadership serves the life of the community rather than dominating it. Those who guide are also guided by the same law that shapes everyone else. This creates unity within structure.

The people begin to understand that leadership within their community is not a position of separation but a place of service. Authority and responsibility work together to maintain the health of the community.

Community reflecting divine intention

As these elements come together, a picture begins to form. The community is being shaped into something that reflects God's intention for human life. Justice, care, order, and responsibility all become visible expressions of a deeper reality.

The law is not only forming individuals. It is forming a shared life. The people begin to live in a way that reflects the character of the One who brought them out of Egypt. Their community becomes a space where divine intention is made visible in everyday life.

A scholar notes, "The social instructions of the Sinai tradition function as a blueprint for covenant community life in which justice and care reflect the character of God within society."[19] This insight captures how deeply social life is shaped by covenant instruction.

The section closes with a sense of unfolding clarity. The people are no longer only a group that was delivered. They are becoming a community shaped by justice, care, order, and responsibility. Their shared life begins to reflect the presence and purpose of God among them.

---

[19] Bruce Wells, "Social Justice in the Covenant Code," *Journal for the Study of the Old Testament* 33, no. 4 (2009): 412.

Ethical Witness

As the life of Israel takes shape at Sinai, something quietly begins to extend beyond the boundaries of the community itself. What they live, how they speak, how they treat one another, and how they respond to God begins to carry meaning that others can observe. Their life becomes more than private obedience. It becomes a visible testimony. The Bible later captures this expectation when it speaks of them as a light among the nations (Isaiah 49:6). Even at this stage, that direction is already forming.

Conduct revealing identity

Identity that is received at Sinai does not remain hidden. It becomes visible through conduct. The way the people live begins to reflect what they have received. Their actions begin to speak as clearly as their words.

When honesty is practiced in trade, when justice is upheld in disputes, and when care is extended to the vulnerable, something deeper than social order is being expressed. Their conduct begins to reveal who they belong to.

In a small island community in the Pacific region, a group of families once agreed to rebuild their shared spaces after a natural disaster. Their work was simple, but consistent. Over time, neighboring communities began to notice the unity and care they showed toward one another. Without formal messages, their actions communicated something powerful. In a similar way, Israel's conduct begins to reveal their identity.

Witness through daily life

Witness does not begin with speeches. It begins with daily life. The ordinary patterns of living become the place where testimony is formed. The rhythm of work, rest, worship, and relationships all carry meaning.

In Deuteronomy 4:6, the people are later described in a way that reflects this reality: their life of obedience is meant to be observed by others, who will recognize wisdom and understanding among them. This suggests that their daily life carries a teaching function beyond their own community.

In a farming region of East Africa, agricultural practices introduced by a small cooperative became a model for surrounding villages. The change did not come through instruction alone but through visible results in daily work. In a similar way, Israel's life begins to function as a visible testimony through ordinary living.

Influence beyond boundaries

The life of the community does not remain enclosed within itself. As they move through history, their actions begin to influence those around them. Their way of living becomes known beyond their immediate boundaries.

This influence is not forced. It emerges through consistency and integrity. The surrounding nations begin to observe a different pattern of life shaped by justice, worship, and relationship with God.

The presence of such a community within history creates awareness. It draws attention to a way of life that is not defined only by human systems. Their influence begins to extend beyond what they may have imagined at Sinai.

Integrity shaping perception

Integrity becomes one of the strongest forms of witness. When actions align with identity, perception begins to change. The way others see the community is shaped by the consistency of their life.

Integrity does not depend on public moments alone. It is formed in private decisions, in daily interactions, and in unseen choices. Over time, this consistency builds trust and recognition among those who observe them.

In a historic trading route in Central Asia, merchants once became known for their consistent honesty in exchange and agreement. Their reputation spread across regions, not through declarations, but through reliable conduct. In a deeper sense, Israel's integrity begins to shape how they are perceived among the nations.

Invitation through visible life

The life of the community becomes an invitation. Without direct proclamation, their way of living begins to raise questions in those who observe them. Their distinctiveness creates curiosity. Their order, justice, and worship point toward something beyond themselves.

This invitation is not forced. It arises naturally from visibility. A life shaped by God becomes a point of reflection for others. The nations begin to encounter, through Israel, something that speaks beyond human systems.

A scholar reflects on this dynamic by noting, "Israel's covenantal life functions as a public witness in which ethical practice becomes a means through which the knowledge of God is made visible among the nations."[20] This observation captures the outward movement of their identity.

The chapter concludes with a clear progression. The people who were redeemed now live in a way that reveals God to others. Their identity, formed through covenant and law, becomes visible through action. Their life stands as a witness that extends beyond themselves, preparing the way for the unfolding story of Israel within the wider world of history.

---

[20] Walter Moberly, "Ethics and Witness in the Sinai Tradition," *Scottish Journal of Theology* 55, no. 3 (2002): 318.

CHAPTER 5 — LAND, SETTLEMENT, AND VOCATIONAL TENSION

The narrative that once moved through promise, covenant, redemption, and structured formation now enters a new phase where identity is no longer shaped in movement alone but in settled space. The transition into land introduces a different kind of challenge, where fulfillment is experienced alongside complexity. What was once anticipated through journey now becomes lived reality within geography, society, and daily patterns of survival and growth. The land is received as gift, yet it also becomes the environment in which vocation must now be sustained over time.

Within this settled existence, tension begins to surface between inherited calling and evolving conditions of life. Stability brings opportunity for development, but also introduces pressures of adaptation, influence, and gradual shift in focus. Identity is no longer tested only through external opposition, but through internal adjustment within established environments. This chapter traces how settlement reshapes the understanding of vocation, where continuity of purpose must now be maintained within the ordinary rhythms of land, culture, and communal life.

Entry into Land

The journey that began with a call in distant memory now reaches a moment of visible fulfillment. A people who once moved through uncertainty and wilderness now stand at the threshold of a defined geography. The land is before them, not as an abstract promise, but as a lived reality waiting to be entered. The Bible describes this moment with a sense of continuity, where what was spoken long before begins to take form in history (Joshua 1:2–3).

Arrival into promised geography

Entry into the land is not sudden or detached. It is the result of a long unfolding story. The people arrive carrying memory, expectation, and experience. The geography they step into is already shaped in their imagination through generations of promise and anticipation.

As they cross into this space, something shifts in their collective awareness. The land is real, visible, and shared. Hills, rivers, and cities become part of their new environment. What was once spoken to Abraham as distant promise now becomes their immediate reality.

In the foothills of the Himalayan region, migrating communities often speak of the moment they settle after long movement. The landscape feels different when it becomes home rather than passage. The same terrain that once symbolized journey now becomes place of belonging. In a deeper way, Israel begins to experience geography as fulfillment.

Fulfillment of earlier promise

The entry into the land carries the weight of earlier words spoken in covenant and promise. What was declared across generations begins to take shape in lived history. The movement from promise to presence is now visible.

Yet fulfillment is not presented as completion of all movement. It is fulfillment within unfolding purpose. The land is given, but its meaning continues to develop through how it is lived in. The people step into something received, yet still forming.

This moment echoes earlier words spoken to Abraham about land and future generations (Genesis 12:7). What was once distant becomes immediate, yet still connected to a larger narrative that continues beyond this point.

Transition from movement to residence

The shift from wilderness to land is also a shift from movement to residence. In the wilderness, life was shaped by dependence and daily provision. Movement defined identity. Now, stability begins to take form. Settling introduces new patterns of life.

Residency changes perception. The rhythm of travel gives way to rhythm of cultivation, building, and establishing community life. The people begin to experience time differently. Instead of moving toward a destination each day, they begin to shape life within a place.

In a pastoral region of East Africa, nomadic families who transition into settled living often describe a change in how they understand time and responsibility. Movement gives way to planning, cultivation, and shared space. Israel begins to enter a similar transition, where residence becomes part of identity formation.

Memory of wilderness shaping perception

Even as they settle, memory does not disappear. The experience of wilderness remains present within their understanding of the land. Dependence, provision, and guidance continue to shape how they interpret their new environment.

This memory becomes a stabilizing force. It reminds them that the land is gift, not achievement. The same presence that guided them through the wilderness is now present within settlement. Memory prevents the land from becoming only possession. It keeps it within the context of relationship.

The book of Deuteronomy later reflects this awareness when it calls the people to remember the journey through the wilderness as part of understanding their present life (Deuteronomy 8:2). Memory becomes part of identity within the land.

Land as gift and responsibility

The land is received as gift, yet it also introduces responsibility. It is not simply a place of arrival. It becomes a space where life must be shaped in accordance with covenant purpose. Gift carries expectation of response.

The people begin to learn that living in the land involves care, attention, and alignment with the One who gave it. Agriculture, community life, and worship all become expressions of how the gift is received and lived. The land is not neutral space. It is relational space.

A scholar observes, "The entrance into the land in Joshua traditions functions as the historical realization of promise, where gift and responsibility converge in covenantal life."[21] This perspective captures the tension present in this moment of transition.

The section closes with a sense of movement forward. The people who once journeyed without fixed location now stand

---

[21] L. Daniel Hawk, "Land, Promise, and Identity in Joshua," *Catholic Biblical Quarterly* 68, no. 1 (2006): 74.

within a defined land. Their life is shaped by fulfillment, memory, and responsibility. The journey continues, now within geography, where promise meets daily reality.

Settlement Patterns

The land that was entered in fulfillment of promise begins to take shape through everyday living. What once was a unified movement of a traveling people now unfolds into patterns of settlement. Life begins to spread across regions, valleys, and hill country. The people do not remain in one place. They begin to organize themselves within space, forming communities that reflect both their shared identity and the realities of geography.

Distribution among regions

As the people settle, land is not experienced in a single uniform way. Different regions shape different ways of living. Some areas support agriculture, others support livestock, and others become centers of gathering and trade.

This distribution is not random. It reflects both opportunity and necessity. Families and tribes begin to locate themselves in areas where life can be sustained. Over time, geography begins to influence rhythm of life. The land becomes part of identity formation.

In parts of East Africa, pastoral groups often settle in patterns that follow water sources and grazing land. These patterns slowly shape social structure and community interaction. In a similar way, Israel begins to experience settlement as a response to both environment and shared life.

Development of local communities

Within these regions, smaller communities begin to form. Life becomes more localized. Neighbors share resources, responsibilities, and daily concerns. The larger identity of the people is now expressed through local interaction.

These communities are shaped by proximity and shared necessity. Relationships grow through daily work, seasonal cycles, and communal responsibilities. The sense of belonging becomes more tangible in smaller social spaces.

What began as a unified journey now becomes a network of connected communities. Each one carries the same covenant identity, yet expresses it within different local settings.

Agricultural and economic life

Settlement introduces a new relationship with land. Agriculture becomes central to daily survival. Fields are cultivated, harvests are gathered, and seasons begin to shape expectation. Economic life begins to form around production and exchange.

This shift changes how time is experienced. Instead of movement through wilderness, life is now shaped by cycles of planting and harvesting. Dependence on land becomes visible in daily activity. The people begin to learn that stability requires care and attention.

In rural regions of South Asia, farming communities often describe how their understanding of time changes once they settle into agricultural life. Seasons become markers of expectation and responsibility. In a similar way, Israel begins to structure life around rhythms of land and labor.

Family and tribal organization

Within settlement, family and tribal structures take on new importance. Households become centers of daily life. Larger tribal identity provides connection across regions. These structures offer stability within geographic dispersion.

Families carry responsibility for land, work, and social relationships. Tribes maintain connection to shared history and covenant identity. Together, they form a layered structure of belonging.

This organization allows the people to remain connected even as they live in different regions. Identity is preserved through both family memory and tribal continuity.

Stability within geographic presence

As settlement develops, a sense of stability begins to emerge. The people are no longer moving toward a future location. They are now living within it. This stability creates space for development of culture, practice, and social life.

Yet stability is not final. It remains shaped by memory of journey and promise. The people carry within them the awareness that their identity is still rooted in covenant rather than geography alone.

A scholar notes, “Settlement in the land functions as a social transformation in which tribal and regional organization becomes the lived expression of covenant identity within geographic space."[22] This observation captures how deeply life is shaped by settlement patterns.

The section closes with a sense of unfolding order. The people are no longer only recipients of land. They are now builders of community within it. Their life takes shape through regions, relationships, and rhythms of work, forming a structured presence within the land they have entered.

Faithfulness and Instability

Life in the land brings a new kind of tension. The people are no longer wandering, yet they are not settled in a way that removes struggle. Within the stability of geography, another movement begins quietly. Memory of covenant instructions remains present, yet daily life introduces pressures that pull in different directions. Faithfulness becomes something lived over time, shaped by decisions, influences, and changing circumstances.

Memory of covenant instructions

Even in settlement, the people carry memory. The instructions given at Sinai are not forgotten. They remain part of their identity, shaping how they understand worship, justice, and community life. Memory becomes a guiding presence within ordinary decisions.

This memory is often recalled in moments of decision making, especially when life becomes complex. It serves as a reminder of who they are and what they have received. Yet memory alone does not determine action. It exists alongside other forces that influence daily life.

In many traditional communities across East Asia, elders often preserve oral memory of foundational agreements that shaped their villages. These memories guide decisions even when new circumstances arise. In a similar way, Israel's covenant memory continues to speak within the changing environment of settlement.

Pressure of surrounding influences

As the people live among different cultures and neighboring societies, influence becomes part of daily experience.

---

[22] Norman K. Gottwald, "Early Israelite Settlement Patterns and Social Formation," *Journal of Biblical Literature* 101, no. 4 (1982): 521.

Trade, interaction, and proximity introduce new practices and ideas. These influences are not always negative in appearance, yet they carry the potential to reshape identity.

The land is shared space. As interaction increases, distinction becomes more challenging to maintain. The people begin to negotiate their identity within a broader cultural environment. This creates internal pressure between memory and adaptation.

In a trading region of Central Asia, communities along historic routes often absorbed elements of surrounding cultures while maintaining core identity. Over time, some groups remained distinct while others gradually shifted in practice. Israel begins to experience a similar tension within its settled life.

Cycles of obedience and failure

Within this environment, the people experience cycles. There are moments of faithfulness, where life aligns with covenant memory. There are also moments of failure, where influence and circumstance lead in different directions. These cycles become part of their lived reality.

Faithfulness is not presented as a fixed state. It becomes a repeated movement of return and drift. This rhythm shapes the spiritual life of the community. The tension between obedience and failure becomes part of their ongoing story within the land.

In many rural communities across Africa, seasonal changes often bring cycles of discipline and lapse in communal agreements, especially when external pressures increase. Over time, communities learn to renew commitment through shared reflection. Israel begins to experience similar patterns within its covenant life.

Spiritual consistency within change

Despite instability, something remains steady. The presence of God and the memory of covenant continue to anchor identity. Even when actions vary, the foundational relationship remains. This creates space for restoration and renewal within the life of the people.

Spiritual consistency does not mean absence of struggle. It means that even within change, there is a continuing reference point. The people are not abandoned to instability. They are held within a relationship that continues to call them back.

The biblical narrative often reflects this movement, where failure is met with renewed instruction and return. This rhythm becomes part of how identity is preserved within history.

Struggle for sustained identity

Over time, the central challenge becomes clear. The people struggle to maintain sustained identity within changing conditions. Memory, influence, obedience, and failure all interact within their lived experience. Identity is not lost, but it is constantly tested.

This struggle shapes the deeper meaning of settlement. Life in the land is not only about possession. It is about continuity of calling within complexity. The people are learning that identity must be carried through time, not only received in a moment.

A scholar observes, "The settlement period in early Israel reflects a dynamic tension between covenant memory and socio-cultural adaptation, producing cycles of fidelity and instability within communal identity."[23] This insight captures the lived complexity of this stage.

The section closes with awareness of tension. The people who entered the land now live within a rhythm of faithfulness and instability. Their identity remains grounded in covenant memory, yet their experience continues to be shaped by surrounding life. The story moves forward within this tension, preparing for deeper questions of identity and direction.

Cultural Interaction

Life in the land does not develop in isolation. Settlement places the people within a shared world where neighboring groups, trade routes, and regional practices intersect. The land becomes a space of interaction, where identity is shaped not only by internal memory but also by external contact. What was once a separated journey now becomes a lived experience within a broader human environment.

Contact with neighboring cultures

As the people settle, contact with surrounding nations becomes part of ordinary life. Through trade, travel, and proximity, different cultures meet. These encounters are not

---

[23] John Van Seters, "The Problem of Historical Continuity in Early Israel," *Vetus Testamentum* 34, no. 2 (1984): 193.

always dramatic. Often they occur in daily exchange, shared markets, and regional cooperation.

Such contact introduces new ways of speaking, working, and organizing life. It creates awareness of difference while also revealing shared human patterns. The land becomes a meeting place of multiple identities living side by side.

In regions of North Africa, historical caravan routes connected communities across deserts and cities. Over time, local traditions absorbed certain practices while maintaining core identity. In a similar way, Israel begins to encounter cultural exchange as part of settled life.

Exchange of practices and ideas

Interaction leads naturally to exchange. Ideas about agriculture, craftsmanship, governance, and social organization move across communities. Some of these practices are adopted, others are resisted, and many are adapted into existing life.

This exchange creates both enrichment and tension. It introduces possibilities for development, but also raises questions about identity. What should be received and what should be preserved becomes a lived discernment within community life.

In a river basin region of Southeast Asia, agricultural communities historically shared irrigation methods across cultural boundaries. While techniques were exchanged, each group maintained distinct social and spiritual identity. Israel begins to experience similar dynamics within its settled geography.

Influence on worship and lifestyle

Cultural interaction also affects deeper areas of life, including worship and daily practice. As different forms of religious expression become visible, questions arise about alignment with covenant identity. The surrounding environment introduces patterns that may appear attractive or familiar.

This creates a space of discernment. Worship and lifestyle become areas where identity is tested through exposure. The people must continually remember what defines their relationship with God while living in a shared cultural environment.

In many ancient Mediterranean societies, religious practices often overlapped through regional influence, leading communities to negotiate boundaries of worship and identity.

Israel's experience reflects a similar challenge within its settled context.

Boundaries of identity in interaction

Within this shared space, boundaries become important. Identity is not preserved by separation alone, but by conscious living. The people begin to understand that interaction does not require absorption. It requires discernment.

Boundaries are not presented as barriers to life with others. They function as markers of identity. Through them, the people maintain clarity about who they are while engaging meaningfully with surrounding cultures.

These dynamic shapes daily decisions, from social relationships to communal practices. Identity becomes something actively maintained within interaction rather than passively preserved.

Shared space with difference

Ultimately, the land is revealed as shared space. Different peoples live within proximity, each carrying distinct histories and practices. Difference becomes part of the environment rather than an exception to it.

The presence of multiple cultures within the same geography creates a complex social reality. It requires wisdom, awareness, and continual reflection on identity. The people of Israel are learning how to live faithfully within this shared world without losing their distinct calling.

A scholar notes, "Early Israelite settlement must be understood within a context of cultural interaction in which identity formation occurs through both exchange and resistance in shared geographic space."[24] This observation reflects the complexity of life within the land.

The section closes with recognition of ongoing tension. The people are no longer isolated. They are participants in a wider world of cultures and influences. Their identity continues to develop within interaction, preparing the narrative for deeper questions of direction and purpose in the land.

---

[24] Mark S. Smith, "Culture and Identity in Early Israel," *Journal of Ancient Near Eastern Studies* 45, no. 2 (2008): 201.

Vocational Drift

As life in the land continues, something subtle begins to unfold within the community. The people are no longer in transition. They are settled, organized, and engaged in daily life shaped by geography and culture. Yet within this stability, a quiet movement begins. The original sense of calling that once defined identity starts to lose clarity. This shift is gradual, almost unnoticeable at first, yet it reshapes how life is understood and lived.

Gradual loss of focus on covenant purpose

The memory of covenant purpose does not disappear, but it begins to fade at the edges of daily concern. Survival, productivity, and local stability slowly take center stage. The larger sense of vocation that once defined the people begins to feel less immediate.

This does not happen through rejection. It happens through gradual reordering of priorities. As life becomes more settled, immediate needs begin to shape attention. Over time, focus shifts from calling to continuity of daily life.

In many rural communities that transition from migration to settlement, early generational memory of movement and purpose often weakens as new generations grow within stability. The story of origin becomes background rather than guiding center. Israel begins to experience a similar transition within its settled life.

Attraction of alternative identities

As interaction with surrounding cultures increases, alternative ways of defining identity become visible. These are not always presented as replacements. They often appear as additional options for living, organizing, and belonging.

Over time, the attraction of these alternatives creates quiet tension. The people begin to see other models of life that appear stable, successful, or socially integrated. This introduces the possibility of reshaping identity in ways that differ from original calling.

In coastal trading societies of the Indian Ocean, communities historically adapted aspects of multiple cultures through commerce and interaction. While this created richness, it also led in some cases to gradual blending of identity markers.

Israel begins to face similar pressures within its geographic and cultural setting.

Shift from vocation to survival patterns

One of the most significant changes in settled life is the shift from vocation-centered living to survival-centered patterns. Daily life becomes focused on maintaining stability, securing resources, and managing local demands.

Vocation, once understood as participation in a larger divine purpose, begins to feel secondary to immediate concerns. This shift does not occur through deliberate abandonment. It develops through repeated decisions shaped by necessity and environment.

Over time, survival patterns begin to define rhythm of life more strongly than calling. This creates a quiet displacement of purpose within ordinary living.

Internal weakening of distinctiveness

As these changes continue, distinctiveness begins to weaken internally. The people still carry identity markers, yet their expression becomes less clear. The boundaries that once defined them begin to blur in daily practice and interaction.

This weakening is not immediate or visible in dramatic form. It is gradual and relational. It appears in small adjustments, shared practices, and shifting priorities. Identity becomes less sharply defined within lived experience.

In many ancient societies, cultural identity often softened over generations of interaction and settlement, especially when external influences became part of everyday life. Israel begins to experience similar internal pressures within its settled environment.

Need for renewed direction

Within this unfolding tension, a deeper need begins to emerge. The people require renewed clarity of direction. Memory alone is no longer sufficient to sustain identity. Life within settlement requires continual reorientation toward original calling.

This need does not suggest abandonment of covenant purpose. It highlights the necessity of renewal within ongoing history. The people are still within promise, still within land, yet they require moments of re-centering to remain aligned with their vocation.

A scholar observes, “Vocational identity in early Israelite settlement demonstrates a gradual tension between inherited purpose and adaptive survival structures, requiring continual processes of communal reorientation.”[25] This insight captures the slow movement of drift within settled life.

The section closes with awareness of subtle transition. The people who once lived with clear sense of calling now experience the complexity of sustained settlement. Their vocation remains present, yet it requires renewed attention. This prepares the narrative for future movements of reflection, correction, and restoration within their history.

[25] Susan Niditch, “Tradition and Transformation in Early Israelite Identity,” *Harvard Theological Review* 94, no. 3 (2001): 287.

CHAPTER 6 — MONARCHY, WORSHIP, AND FAILURE

As the settled life of the people develops into a more organized national structure, a new phase emerges where identity becomes increasingly shaped by centralized leadership and institutional systems. The rise of monarchy introduces a visible form of governance that seeks to unify direction, stabilize authority, and give coherence to the life of the nation. What had been distributed across tribes and regions begins to gather around royal leadership, marking a significant shift in how collective identity is expressed and maintained.

Alongside this structural development, worship also begins to take more defined and institutional form, linking religious life more closely with national order. Yet within this consolidation of authority and practice, tensions begin to surface between intended direction and lived reality. Strength of structure does not remove vulnerability, and organization does not eliminate distortion. This chapter follows how monarchy and worship develop together, while also revealing how internal weakness gradually emerges within systems designed to preserve unity and purpose.

Rise of Kingship

The story of Israel now enters a new layer of social organization. A people who once moved through calling, covenant, redemption, law, land, and settlement now begin to seek visible structure in leadership. Life in the land has grown complex. Tribal systems that once held community life together begin to feel stretched across time, conflict, and competing demands. Within this context, the desire for centralized leadership emerges as a response to national complexity and internal tension.

Transition from tribal leadership to monarchy

In earlier stages, leadership was distributed. Tribal elders, judges, and shared responsibilities guided the life of the people. This form of leadership carried flexibility and closeness to daily life. Yet as settlement expanded and regional differences increased, coordination became more difficult.

Over time, the need for a more unified form of leadership begins to surface. The people begin to imagine stability through a single governing figure who can represent national identity and provide consistent direction. This marks the gradual movement from shared tribal leadership toward monarchy.

In many historical societies, transitions from tribal systems to centralized rule often emerge when communities expand beyond local cohesion. In parts of pre-modern Southeast Asia, village-based leadership structures gradually gave way to centralized kingdoms as trade, conflict, and population growth increased. A similar structural transition begins to appear within Israel's historical development.

Desire for structured national governance

As life becomes more complex, the desire for structured governance increases. Disputes between regions, external threats, and internal inconsistency create a longing for unified authority. Leadership is now seen not only as guidance but also as organization of national life.

This desire reflects a deeper search for stability. The people are no longer only concerned with survival or settlement. They now seek coherence across their entire national experience. Governance becomes a way to hold identity together across geography and social diversity.

The longing for structure is not simply political. It is also social and psychological. A unified center of authority promises clarity in a world that is becoming increasingly layered and complex.

Appointment and authority of kings

With the rise of kingship, authority becomes more defined and concentrated. The king becomes a visible representation of national unity. Leadership is no longer dispersed among tribal figures alone but gathered into a singular institutional role.

This appointment introduces a new dynamic. Authority now carries both administrative and symbolic weight. The king represents order, direction, and identity for the people. His role extends beyond governance into shaping national imagination.

In ancient Near Eastern cultures, kingship often functioned as both political and symbolic leadership, where rulers were seen as stabilizing figures of national identity. Israel's adoption of kingship follows a similar historical pattern, while carrying its own covenant context.

Shift from shared leadership to centralized rule

The movement toward monarchy also represents a shift in how leadership is experienced. Shared leadership allows multiple voices and regional participation. Centralized rule gathers decision-making into one point of authority.

This shift changes the rhythm of national life. Decision-making becomes faster and more unified, yet also more dependent on a single leadership structure. The balance between distributed responsibility and centralized authority begins to change.

This transition affects how the people relate to governance itself. Leadership becomes something external and centralized rather than fully embedded within shared tribal participation.

Expectation of stability through kingship

At the heart of this transition lies expectation. The people anticipate that centralized leadership will bring stability, unity, and protection. Kingship is seen as a solution to fragmentation and inconsistency experienced within earlier structures.

This expectation shapes how monarchy is received. It is not only an administrative change. It is a hope for coherence in national life. The king becomes a symbol of stability in a complex and shifting environment.

Yet beneath this expectation lies an ongoing question about how stability will interact with covenant identity. Leadership now carries the responsibility of holding together both governance and spiritual direction within a single structure.

A scholar observes, "The emergence of monarchy in ancient Israel reflects a socio-political consolidation in response to tribal fragmentation and external pressure, producing a centralized model of leadership that reshaped national identity."[26] This perspective captures the historical weight of this transition.

---

[26] Susan Niditch, "The Emergence of Kingship in Early Israel," *Journal of Biblical Literature* 102, no. 3 (1983): 319.

The section closes with awareness of a turning point. The people who once lived under distributed tribal leadership now begin to gather around centralized authority. Kingship emerges as a response to complexity, reshaping governance, identity, and expectation. The narrative continues forward into deeper questions of political identity and institutional life.

Political Identity

With the rise of kingship, a deeper layer of identity begins to take shape within the life of the people. What was once defined through tribes, shared memory, and covenant belonging now begins to express itself through national structure. The people slowly come to understand themselves as one organized body under a unified political order. Identity is no longer only inherited; it is now also formed through governance and visible leadership.

Development of unified political structure

The establishment of monarchy brings a new sense of national cohesion. Tribal distinctions remain, yet a broader structure begins to gather the people into a single political body. Governance becomes more coordinated, and collective decisions begin to reflect national unity rather than regional independence.

This development is clearly reflected when the people request a king, saying they desire to be like other nations (1 Samuel 8:5). The request reveals more than political preference. It expresses a desire for visible structure that defines national existence in a way comparable to surrounding societies.

Over time, political structure becomes the framework through which unity is experienced. The nation begins to function as a single entity under centralized leadership, rather than as loosely connected tribal groups.

National identity shaped by leadership

As monarchy becomes established, leadership begins to shape national self-understanding. The king is not only a governing figure but also a symbol of collective identity. Through him, the people begin to see themselves as a unified nation rather than a scattered set of families.

When David is established as king over all Israel, the narrative highlights that his rule confirms national unity under divine appointment (2 Samuel 5:12). Leadership and identity become closely intertwined, and the nation begins to define itself through the structure of kingship.

This connection reshapes imagination and belonging. The people now carry a political identity that is expressed through leadership, institution, and national continuity.

Relationship between people and king

A new relational dynamic emerges between the people and the king. The king becomes a central figure through whom national life is organized and represented. Leadership is no longer dispersed but concentrated in a visible authority that carries responsibility for the nation.

This relationship involves expectation and accountability. The king is called to lead in justice and direction, while the people participate in national life under his governance. The bond between ruler and community becomes a defining feature of political identity.

Samuel's address to the people highlights this shared responsibility within national structure, where both leadership and response shape the stability of the nation (1 Samuel 12:14).

Influence of surrounding political models

Political identity develops within a wider regional context. Neighboring nations already function under established monarchies, and their systems influence how kingship is understood. Israel's emerging political identity is formed in conversation with these external models.

The desire to adopt similar structures is explicitly expressed when the people ask for a king so they may be like other nations (1 Samuel 8:20). This reflects the natural influence of surrounding political frameworks on internal development.

As a result, Israel's political identity carries both continuity with covenant history and adaptation to regional political realities.

Integration of governance and identity

Over time, governance becomes closely integrated with identity. The structure of leadership is no longer external to the people's sense of self. It becomes part of how the nation understands its existence and purpose in history.

Political organization, leadership, and national unity begin to function together as expressions of collective identity. The king represents both authority and national coherence.

Earlier covenant instruction already anticipated kingship within a framework of divine guidance (Deuteronomy 17:15). Within the monarchy, this structure becomes visible in lived national experience, where governance and identity are closely connected. In this context, Mark A. O'Brien notes, "Israel's political identity under monarchy reflects a developing consciousness shaped through centralized leadership while interacting with surrounding state models and inherited covenant memory."[27]

The people who once defined themselves through tribal belonging and covenant memory now experience identity through political structure. National consciousness begins to take visible form through kingship, preparing the narrative for the next movement into worship and institutional life.

Worship and Structure

As monarchy becomes established, worship also begins to take a more structured form within national life. What was once expressed through shared memory, tribal participation, and movable sacred gatherings now begins to be organized within defined spaces, patterns, and leadership structures. Worship is no longer only a spontaneous expression of covenant life. It becomes part of national order, shaped alongside political development and institutional stability.

Centralization of worship practices

One of the most significant developments in this period is the movement toward centralization of worship. Instead of multiple local expressions, worship begins to gather around designated places where the presence of God is acknowledged in a national setting.

This movement is reflected in the establishment of central worship locations such as Shiloh in earlier periods (1 Samuel 1:3), and later developments toward a more unified place of worship

[27] Mark A. O'Brien, "Kingship and Identity Formation in Ancient Israel," *Catholic Biblical Quarterly* 62, no. 4 (2000): 587.

during the monarchy. The centralization of worship reflects the desire for unity not only in governance but also in spiritual life.

Deuteronomy 12:5 points toward the idea of a chosen place where worship is to be gathered, indicating that worship was gradually being shaped into a unified national expression rather than scattered local practices.

Development of institutional worship spaces

As worship becomes centralized, physical and institutional spaces begin to take clearer form. Sacred spaces are no longer only temporary or tribal in nature. They become established locations where worship is organized and maintained.

The construction of Solomon's temple represents a defining moment in this development (1 Kings 6:1). Worship is now associated with a permanent structure that reflects national identity and continuity. The temple becomes a focal point where prayer, sacrifice, and national gathering converge.

This development shows how worship and national life begin to share the same visible structure. Sacred space becomes part of the identity of the nation.

Role of leadership in religious expression

With the rise of monarchy, leadership begins to play a significant role in shaping worship practices. Kings are involved in national religious expression, influencing how worship is organized and maintained.

David's involvement in bringing the ark to Jerusalem (2 Samuel 6:12–15) demonstrates how political leadership intersects with worship life. The king participates in worship as part of national identity, and his actions shape how the people engage with sacred practices.

Leadership becomes a bridge between national governance and religious life, integrating both dimensions within the structure of society.

Standardization of rituals and practices

As worship becomes institutionalized, rituals and practices begin to take more defined and consistent forms. Sacrificial systems, festivals, and communal observances develop patterns that guide collective participation.

These patterns provide continuity across generations. Leviticus 23 outlines appointed times and structured observances, showing how worship is organized within a shared rhythm of national life.

Standardization helps maintain unity across regions and communities. Worship becomes a shared language that expresses collective identity through repeated practice.

Connection between worship and national order

Worship in this period is closely connected to national structure. It is not separate from governance or social organization. Instead, it functions as part of the overall order of society.

When worship is aligned with national life, it reinforces unity and shared identity. When it is neglected or distorted, it affects the stability of the community as a whole. This connection is visible throughout the narrative of Israel's monarchy, where spiritual condition and national condition often move together (1 Kings 11:4–6). Frank H. Polak writes, "In monarchic Israel, worship becomes increasingly centralized and structured, reflecting the integration of religious practice within the broader framework of state formation"[28]

The development of structured worship marks a significant stage in Israel's national life. Sacred practices are now organized within institutional systems that reflect both unity and complexity. Worship becomes part of how the nation understands itself, how it gathers, and how it expresses its identity before God and within history.

Institutional Strength and Weakness

As the life of the nation becomes more structured under monarchy, new systems begin to emerge that organize governance, worship, and social life. Administration takes clearer shape, leadership becomes more defined, and national processes gain stability. At the same time, this development introduces a subtle tension between organized strength and lived reality. What brings order also creates distance, and what builds efficiency also tests authenticity.

Stability through structured governance

---

[28] Frank H. Polak, "Social Dimensions of Worship in Ancient Israel," *Vetus Testamentum* 54, no. 2 (2004): 213.

The formation of institutional systems brings a sense of stability to national life. Decisions are no longer scattered or delayed through fragmented tribal processes. Governance becomes more coordinated, allowing the nation to function with clearer direction and continuity.

This stability is reflected in the administrative reforms and organized leadership structures seen during the monarchy, particularly in periods of centralized governance under kings such as Solomon, where administrative divisions and structured oversight were introduced (1 Kings 4:7–19). The system allowed the nation to function with remarkable order across regions.

Structured governance provides clarity. Laws, responsibilities, and leadership roles become more defined, helping the nation maintain coherence in its growing complexity.

Efficiency in national organization

With institutional development comes efficiency. Systems of taxation, leadership delegation, and regional administration begin to support national function. Tasks that once required local negotiation are now managed through organized channels of authority.

This efficiency strengthens national capacity. Resources are coordinated, infrastructure is developed, and governance becomes more capable of sustaining large-scale society. The structured system allows the nation to respond more effectively to internal and external demands.

However, efficiency also begins to reshape how people relate to authority. Interaction becomes mediated through systems rather than direct relational structures.

Emergence of administrative systems

As monarchy matures, administrative systems become more visible. Officials, governors, and appointed leaders begin to manage various aspects of national life. This includes economic management, judicial processes, and regional oversight.

The presence of such systems reflects growing complexity within the nation. Leadership is no longer concentrated in a single personal relationship but distributed through organized institutional frameworks.

In earlier periods, leadership often operated through direct relational engagement. Now, governance increasingly functions through structured mechanisms that extend across the land.

Vulnerability to internal distortion

Alongside strength, institutional systems also carry vulnerability. Over time, structures that were intended to serve life can begin to operate independently of it. The system itself can become more visible than the purpose it was meant to support.

This tension appears in various moments of Israel's history, where administrative and religious systems continue to function while the heart of covenant life weakens. The prophets later speak into this gap, addressing situations where structure remains but authenticity fades (Isaiah 1:11–17).

Micah's reflection captures this tension when he speaks of what is required beyond ritual form, pointing toward justice, mercy, and humility as the deeper expression of covenant life (Micah 6:6–8).

Distance between structure and lived identity

As institutions expand, a gradual distance can emerge between formal structure and lived identity. Systems continue to operate, yet personal and communal experience may begin to drift from the original purpose that shaped them.

This distance does not appear suddenly. It develops slowly through routine, repetition, and institutional layering. What begins as a tool for order can become a separate layer of life if it is no longer connected to the lived reality of the people.

The narrative of Israel shows moments where worship, governance, and social order continue in structured form while the relational depth of covenant life weakens, as reflected in later prophetic observations (Amos 5:21–24).

The life of the nation now carries both strength and strain. Structure provides stability, yet also introduces complexity in how identity is lived. The systems that hold the community together also test the connection between form and meaning, between organization and experience.

Collapse of Direction

As institutional life expands and strengthens, another reality slowly emerges within the national story. The structures that once provided stability begin to reveal cracks in their inner coherence. Leadership continues, worship continues, administration continues, yet the shared sense of direction that once unified the people begins to weaken. What was once a clear movement shaped by calling, covenant, and redemption now starts to feel divided within itself.

Disconnection between leadership and calling

In earlier stages, leadership carried a visible connection to divine calling and covenant purpose. Over time, this connection becomes less consistent. Kings, officials, and institutional leaders begin to operate within political and social pressures that gradually reshape priorities.

This disconnection is visible in moments where leadership decisions diverge from earlier covenant direction. The narrative of Israel records repeated instances where kings lead the people into patterns that no longer reflect their original vocation (1 Kings 12:28–30). The golden calves established in Bethel and Dan illustrate how leadership choices can redirect collective focus away from foundational identity.

When leadership loses alignment with calling, the people experience confusion about direction and purpose.

Fragmentation of covenant awareness

As generations pass, memory of covenant begins to lose its shared clarity. The foundational awareness that once shaped identity becomes uneven across the community. Some remember, some reinterpret, and some gradually forget.

This fragmentation is reflected in the cyclical patterns described throughout the historical narrative, where covenant language remains present but does not always shape daily life (Judges 2:10–12). The awareness of belonging begins to weaken, even while external forms of religious life continue.

Covenant memory, once central to identity, becomes one voice among many within the national experience.

Decline in spiritual and ethical direction

Alongside fragmentation of memory, there is a gradual decline in spiritual and ethical clarity. Practices continue, but alignment with covenant purpose becomes inconsistent. Justice, compassion, and faithfulness begin to appear uneven across national life.

This decline is echoed in prophetic reflections that describe a people who maintain external expressions of worship while losing inner alignment with righteousness (Hosea 4:1–2). The tension between outward form and inward direction becomes increasingly visible.

Ethical life, once shaped by covenant awareness, begins to reflect the complexity of competing influences.

Internal contradictions within national life

As fragmentation deepens, internal contradictions become more apparent. The nation carries both structured worship and social injustice, both institutional order and relational breakdown. These contradictions exist within the same system, revealing tension between form and meaning.

The prophetic voice later describes this condition with striking clarity, where offerings are brought while injustice remains unaddressed (Amos 5:24). The coexistence of order and distortion becomes part of national experience.

These contradictions do not appear as sudden collapse but as gradual accumulation within established systems.

Preparation for crisis and renewal

The weakening of unified direction creates conditions where crisis becomes inevitable. Yet within the same movement, space is also prepared for renewal. The fragmentation of systems exposes the need for deeper restoration that cannot be achieved through structure alone.

This moment in the narrative prepares the ground for prophetic emergence. Voices arise that call the people back to original purpose, reminding them of covenant identity beyond institutional form. The later prophetic tradition stands within this space of tension, calling for return, renewal, and reorientation (Isaiah 55:1–3).

A study on ancient Israel's institutional decline notes that "when centralized systems lose alignment with foundational vocation, internal coherence gives way to fragmented identity, creating conditions for prophetic intervention."[29]

---

[29] Jonathan P. Reed, "Institutional Complexity and Identity Crisis in Ancient Israelite Monarchy," *Journal for the Study of the Old Testament* 29, no. 3 (2005): 317–334.

What begins as unity through structure moves through tension into fragmentation of direction. Yet even within this fragmentation, the larger narrative continues forward, preparing the way for renewal shaped by prophetic insight and restored vision.

Conclusion

The rise of monarchy marks a decisive shift in the life of the people. What once existed as a loosely connected community shaped by covenant memory, redemption, law, and land now begins to take visible form through centralized national structure. Leadership becomes concentrated, governance becomes organized, and worship becomes institutionalized within defined frameworks.

Monarchy brings a new sense of national coherence. The people begin to experience identity through structured authority, unified political systems, and organized religious practice. Kingship provides stability in a complex and expanding society, shaping how the nation functions across regions and generations. This movement is reflected in the transition from tribal governance to centralized rule, where national direction becomes increasingly coordinated under royal leadership (1 Samuel 10:24–25).

Alongside this development, worship also takes structured form. Sacred practices, once expressed through distributed participation, begin to gather within institutional settings that reflect national identity. The temple-centered life of later generations shows how worship and governance become closely aligned within the fabric of society (1 Kings 8:10–13).

Yet within this strengthened structure, an internal tension begins to emerge. Systems that bring order also introduce distance between form and lived reality. The same structures that stabilize national life also reveal vulnerability when disconnected from their original covenantal direction. This tension is visible in moments where institutional strength continues while relational and ethical alignment weakens (2 Kings 17:7–12).

Over time, the movement from shared covenant memory to centralized institutional life creates a gradual shift in how identity is experienced. What was once carried through collective remembrance now becomes mediated through systems of governance and worship. This shift introduces both clarity and complexity, shaping a national identity that is simultaneously strong in structure and fragile in continuity.

A study on ancient Israel's institutional development observes that "the transition from tribal cohesion to centralized monarchy redefined identity through formal systems, yet also introduced structural distance between foundational narrative memory and institutional practice."[30]

This chapter thus marks a turning point in the unfolding narrative. The people who once lived within direct expressions of calling, covenant, redemption, and law now experience their identity through monarchy and institutional worship. The movement carries both advancement and tension, forming the conditions for the emergence of prophetic critique and future renewal.

---

[30] Lester L. Grabbe, "Continuity and Discontinuity in the Development of Israelite Monarchy," *Journal for the Study of the Old Testament* 34, no. 2 (2009): 171–188.

CHAPTER 7 — PROPHETS AND THE GLOBAL HORIZON

As the narrative of Israel moves through monarchy and institutional consolidation, a new form of divine engagement emerges within the same historical space. The prophetic voice arises not outside the system, but within it, bringing interruption to established patterns of political confidence and religious stability. This presence introduces a different kind of awareness, where history is no longer interpreted only through national continuity, but through a living word that challenges, corrects, and reorients the direction of the people.

At the same time, this prophetic movement begins to expand the horizon of understanding beyond internal concerns. The nations that once surrounded Israel as external realities are now drawn into the scope of divine attention, reshaping how history itself is perceived. Judgment, justice, and hope are no longer confined within national boundaries, but begin to reflect a wider field of engagement that includes all peoples. This chapter traces how prophetic speech opens the narrative outward, carrying it from national focus into a broader vision of divine purpose across the world.

Prophetic Intervention

There are moments in history when a settled system continues its rhythm with confidence, yet something within it begins to shift from within rather than from outside. The prophetic movement in Israel enters exactly at this point. The nation still carries its monarchy, its courts, its worship centers, and its administrative order, yet within that ordered life, another voice begins to speak. It does not come from outside the system but rises within it, as if history itself is being addressed from its center.

The emergence of prophetic voice within monarchy is not random. It appears at points where the memory of covenant begins to fade under the weight of political stability. In the days of Samuel, the transition toward kingship already carried tension between divine calling and national desire for structure (1 Samuel 8:7–9). Within that same unfolding system, prophetic voice begins to stand as a reminder that governance alone cannot carry identity. The prophet speaks into the very place where leadership has become secure in itself.

This is why prophetic intervention often occurs within courts, assemblies, and public gatherings. Nathan enters the royal space of David and speaks into the hidden moral fracture of power (2 Samuel 12:1–7). His words do not come from distance but from proximity. The confrontation is not against monarchy as structure alone, but against distortion within responsibility. The narrative does not show a rejection of order, but a reawakening of accountability within it.

In another moment, Elijah appears before Ahab in the context of national crisis and ecological disruption. His presence interrupts the assumed stability of the royal system and redirects attention toward covenant reality (1 Kings 17:1). The drought becomes more than environmental condition; it becomes a theological interruption within national life. Elijah does not stand outside the system but speaks directly into its assumptions, exposing the distance between authority and faithfulness.

Prophets also speak in public spaces where national identity is expressed. Amos addresses gatherings where worship continues while injustice remains embedded in society (Amos 5:21–24). His voice does not reject worship itself but challenges the separation between ritual and righteousness. The prophetic interruption reveals that structured religion without ethical alignment becomes incomplete expression.

Within these moments, confrontation with leadership patterns becomes unavoidable. Kings, officials, and priests are not addressed as outsiders but as participants in a shared covenant history. The prophetic word recalls earlier memory, not as nostalgia but as active identity. When Jeremiah speaks within the temple setting, the message calls the people back to original covenant awareness that has been gradually displaced (Jeremiah 7:3–7). The issue is not absence of worship but misalignment of life.

This movement shows that prophetic speech functions as reorientation rather than replacement. It does not dismantle national life but repositions it. The interruption is internal because the covenant itself is internal to the identity of the people. The voice that enters the system carries continuity with what was spoken earlier in calling, covenant, redemption, and law, yet it brings those foundations into present correction.

A study of prophetic activity in ancient Near Eastern societies notes that "prophetic speech often functioned as an internal corrective mechanism within established political systems, redirecting collective memory toward foundational identity rather than external critique of structure alone."[31]

The emergence of prophetic intervention therefore becomes a moment where divine communication breaks into institutional stability. It does not operate from distance but from within lived history. The interruption is not disorder; it is reorientation. Through this voice, attention is redirected toward original calling, restoring awareness of purpose within a system that has become self-assured.

Justice and Correction

When prophetic voice enters the life of a nation, it does not remain limited to correction of belief or worship alone. It moves directly into the patterns of daily life, where decisions about people, resources, and relationships reveal the true shape of a society. In Israel's prophetic tradition, justice becomes the place where worship and life meet. What is spoken in sacred space is measured by what is practiced in shared space.

Justice as a central concern appears repeatedly in the prophetic message. Isaiah speaks into a society where ritual activity continues, yet human suffering is overlooked. The words echo with a clear interruption: "learn to do right; seek justice" (Isaiah 1:17). The concern is not absence of worship but imbalance between worship and lived responsibility. The prophetic voice does not introduce a new ethic; it restores visibility to what had been neglected within covenant memory.

Amos presents this concern with striking clarity. He speaks into markets, gates, and places of exchange where economic life has become disconnected from moral

---

[31] Robert P. Gordon, "Prophetic Speech as Social Intervention in Ancient Israel," *Journal for the Study of the Old Testament* 41, no. 2 (2016): 213–229.

responsibility. His words expose systems where the vulnerable are overlooked while prosperity continues for others. The declaration, "let justice roll on like a river" (Amos 5:24), is not poetic abstraction but a reordering of public life. Justice is not imagined as occasional action but continuous flow shaping society itself.

The exposure of inequality becomes a recurring theme within prophetic correction. In the vineyard narrative of Naboth, the misuse of authority by Ahab and Jezebel reveals how centralized power can distort inheritance and dignity (1 Kings 21:1–16). The prophetic response does not merely address personal wrongdoing but structural imbalance within governance. Elijah's confrontation stands within this narrative as a reminder that authority carries moral accountability beyond private intention.

Correction also reaches into religious practice when it becomes separated from ethical responsibility. Jeremiah stands at the gate of the temple and declares that security cannot be assumed through ritual presence alone while injustice continues in daily conduct (Jeremiah 7:9–11). Worship and ethical life are not presented as separate spheres. The tension arises when one is maintained while the other is neglected. The prophetic voice restores their unity.

This alignment between worship and social responsibility appears again in Hosea's message, where covenant language is reconnected with relational faithfulness. "I desire mercy, not sacrifice" (Hosea 6:6) becomes a reorientation of religious understanding. The issue is not rejection of worship, but restoration of its meaning within lived relationships. The prophetic correction brings worship back into contact with human reality.

Within this movement, restoration of fairness in communal life becomes visible. The vision is not limited to critique but extends toward rebuilding patterns of interaction where justice is shared rather than concentrated. Ezekiel later reflects this continuity when describing responsibility within community life as measured by fairness and accountability (Ezekiel 18:5–9). The emphasis consistently returns to lived behavior as expression of covenant alignment.

A reflection within recent Old Testament research describes prophetic justice language as "a sustained effort to reconnect ritual expression with social responsibility in order to preserve the integrity of communal identity within ancient Israel."[32]

The prophetic correction therefore operates as ethical recalibration. It does not stand outside society but speaks within it, bringing worship, governance, and daily life back into alignment. Justice becomes the point where spiritual life is measured in visible form, and imbalance is addressed not for disruption alone but for restoration of coherence between belief and action.

Vision Beyond Israel

Prophetic speech in Israel does not remain enclosed within national self-understanding. As the voice of God continues to speak through prophets, the horizon gradually expands beyond internal correction and covenant renewal. What begins as a call to Israel alone begins to open outward, revealing that divine concern is not restricted by geography, ethnicity, or political identity. The prophetic imagination starts to carry the nations within its scope.

This outward movement is not abrupt. It develops through repeated moments where surrounding nations are addressed directly within prophetic speech. The message given to Israel often includes words concerning its neighbors, showing that history is shared space under divine attention.

Surrounding Nations

The prophet Amos begins his message not with Israel, but with surrounding nations such as Damascus, Gaza, Tyre, Edom, Ammon, and Moab (Amos 1:3–2:3). Each nation is addressed with moral language that assumes accountability beyond Israel's borders. The structure of the message itself creates a widening circle of responsibility. Israel is included only after this broader engagement, showing that divine concern is already operating across regional boundaries.

Similarly, Isaiah speaks concerning Egypt and Assyria in a way that includes them within a future of shared

---

[32] Ellen F. Davis, "Justice and Worship in Prophetic Literature," *Catholic Biblical Quarterly* 72, no. 3 (2010): 439.

acknowledgment before God. "In that day Israel will be one of three with Egypt and Assyria, a blessing in the midst of the earth" (Isaiah 19:24). The language does not erase distinction but places former political rivals within a shared horizon of divine purpose.

This inclusion reveals that prophetic speech is not limited to internal national identity. The surrounding world becomes part of the interpretive field of divine activity. Nations are not outside history; they are within it.

Foreign Nations

The prophetic voice also addresses foreign rulers directly. Jeremiah speaks to Babylon through symbolic and direct declarations of accountability (Jeremiah 25:12–14). Even in exile narratives, foreign empires are not beyond the reach of divine communication. Daniel's interaction with Babylonian kings further reflects this pattern, where imperial authority is interpreted within a wider divine framework (Daniel 4:34–37).

Ezekiel expands this even further by addressing Tyre and Egypt in detailed prophetic messages (Ezekiel 28:1–10; 29:1–6). These texts show that prophetic communication moves across political borders without limitation. The assumption underlying these speeches is that no nation exists outside divine awareness or moral accountability.

Even Jonah's narrative introduces this expansion in narrative form. Nineveh, a foreign city outside Israel's covenant structure, becomes the object of prophetic mission (Jonah 3:1–10). The response of the city demonstrates that repentance and divine engagement are not confined to Israel alone. The narrative itself becomes a testimony that divine attention extends outward.

Israel's Role

As prophetic vision expands, Israel's identity is also reinterpreted. The role of Israel is no longer understood as self-contained purpose but as participation within a larger human context. Isaiah articulates this shift clearly when describing Israel as "a light for the nations" (Isaiah 42:6). The identity of the people is defined in relational terms, where their vocation is connected to visibility among other nations.

This does not diminish Israel's identity; it reframes it. Their calling becomes relational rather than exclusive. The purpose of being chosen is connected to representation within a wider human landscape. The prophetic imagination consistently holds Israel within a broader narrative where their life is meant to reflect divine reality to others.

This widening of identity also appears in Psalms where nations are invited into worship. “Declare his glory among the nations” (Psalm 96:3) places Israel’s testimony within a global invitation. The worship of God is envisioned as something that extends beyond internal community life.

Prophetic Language

As prophetic communication develops, its language increasingly includes themes that move beyond internal national concerns. The concern is no longer limited to political stability or ritual correctness within Israel. Instead, prophetic speech begins to describe historical movement that includes multiple nations within divine direction.

Micah envisions a future where “many nations will come and say, come, let us go up to the mountain of the Lord” (Micah 4:2). The image is not restricted to Israel alone but includes a gathering of peoples from diverse backgrounds. The direction of movement is toward shared encounter rather than isolated identity.

Zechariah continues this expansion by describing nations seeking understanding of divine presence through contact with Israel’s life (Zechariah 8:22–23). The language assumes interaction rather than separation, where peoples seek connection through visible expression of divine reality.

Early Movement Toward Global Awareness

Within these prophetic developments, a gradual movement toward global awareness becomes visible. The nations are no longer seen as external to divine purpose but as participants within unfolding history. The prophetic horizon includes multiple peoples within one narrative of accountability and hope.

This movement is not yet fully developed into later mission frameworks, but its direction is clear. The prophetic imagination stretches beyond national boundaries into a shared human future under divine attention. Even in texts like Isaiah 2:2–4, where nations flow toward a common center of instruction, the vision suggests convergence rather than isolation.

A reflection within prophetic literature research notes that "the expansion of prophetic address beyond Israel reflects an emerging perception of history as a shared moral space rather than a collection of isolated national destinies."[33]

The significance of this section lies in its widening perspective. Prophetic communication does not remain fixed within internal correction. It gradually reorients vision toward a larger horizon where nations, history, and divine purpose are understood together. This expansion prepares the narrative for a deeper universal scope and forward-looking orientation in the following sections.

Universal Scope

The prophetic horizon does not stop at national borders or even at regional awareness. As the voice of God continues through the prophets, a deeper conviction emerges: the world itself is held within divine attention. Every people group, every political structure, every act of justice or injustice is brought into a single field of accountability before God. What began as covenant language within Israel gradually opens into a global horizon where humanity is viewed as one moral and historical community under divine oversight.

This expansion does not remove Israel from the narrative. Instead, it places Israel within a wider framework where their story is part of a larger human story. The prophets begin to speak in ways that reveal not only what God is doing for one nation, but what God is doing among all nations.

God's Engagement with All Peoples

One of the clearest signs of universal scope appears in Amos, where God's voice addresses not only Israel but surrounding nations such as Cush, Philistia, Aram, and others (Amos 9:7). The rhetorical question, "Are you not like the Cushites to me, O people of Israel?" (Amos 9:7), redefines assumptions of exclusivity and places all peoples under one divine gaze.

---

[33] Christopher R. Seitz, "The Nations in the Prophets: Expansion of Theological Horizon in Isaiah and Beyond," *Journal of Theological Interpretation* 9, no. 1 (2015): 74.

Isaiah extends this vision further by describing Egypt and Assyria within a shared future of blessing: "Blessed be Egypt my people, Assyria my handiwork, and Israel my inheritance" (Isaiah 19:25). The language places nations historically separated by conflict into one framework of divine recognition. The emphasis rests not on political unity but on shared placement within divine engagement.

This perspective is reinforced in Jonah's narrative, where Nineveh responds to prophetic warning (Jonah 3:5–10). The repentance of a foreign city becomes part of Israel's scriptural memory, showing that divine engagement is not limited to covenant boundaries.

Nations as Part of Moral and Historical Accountability

Prophetic literature consistently presents nations as participants in moral accountability. Jeremiah's message to Babylon includes language of judgment based on historical actions (Jeremiah 25:12–14). The assumption is that empires are not autonomous forces of history but accountable actors within a larger moral order.

Ezekiel speaks against Tyre and Egypt with detailed attention to their economic and political systems (Ezekiel 28:1–8; 29:1–6). These passages reveal that trade, power, and governance are not neutral structures. They are evaluated within a framework of justice and responsibility.

Even Obadiah's brief prophetic message against Edom (Obadiah 1:10–15) demonstrates that historical hostility between nations is not forgotten within divine awareness. Memory itself becomes part of accountability.

Universal Themes of Justice and Restoration

Across prophetic writings, justice is not treated as a local concern but as a universal principle shaping human history. Psalmic reflection calls all nations to recognize divine authority: "Say among the nations, the Lord reigns" (Psalm 96:10). The proclamation assumes a global audience and shared recognition.

Isaiah envisions a time when nations will respond to divine instruction: "Many peoples will come and say, come, let us go up to the mountain of the Lord" (Isaiah 2:3). The direction of movement is outward gathering, where multiple peoples participate in shared instruction.

The theme of restoration also extends beyond Israel. Isaiah speaks of a "new heavens and a new earth" (Isaiah 65:17), a vision that transcends national boundaries and includes the renewal of creation itself.

Shared Human Responsibility under Divine Oversight

Within this expanding vision, human responsibility is no longer confined to one group. The prophets consistently portray humanity as sharing responsibility under divine oversight. Micah's declaration of what is required—"to act justly, love mercy, and walk humbly" (Micah 6:8)—is expressed in universal moral language that applies beyond Israel's internal life.

Daniel's narrative in Babylon reinforces this idea when kings are held accountable for pride, injustice, and misuse of authority (Daniel 4:30–37). The lesson is not restricted to one empire but reveals a principle applied across political systems.

This shared responsibility places all nations within a single moral horizon where actions are not isolated but interconnected within divine awareness.

Expansion of Covenant Language into Global Horizon

Covenant language itself begins to carry outward meaning. The promise that "in you all families of the earth shall be blessed" (Genesis 12:3) becomes increasingly visible within prophetic interpretation. What begins as a promise to Abraham is gradually seen as shaping the destiny of multiple peoples.

Isaiah's language of Israel as "a light to the nations" (Isaiah 49:6) reflects this expansion. Light is not contained within itself; it exists for visibility beyond its source. The covenant identity thus begins to function within a global horizon of purpose.

A recent reflection within prophetic studies notes that "the expansion of divine concern in prophetic literature reflects a theological movement from national identity toward a comprehensive horizon of human accountability within history."[34]

Future Orientation

Prophetic speech never ends in the present moment. Even when it confronts crisis, corruption, or collapse, it carries within

---

[34] Walter Brueggemann, "The Prophetic Imagination and Global Horizon," *Interpretation: A Journal of Bible and Theology* 66, no. 2 (2012): 138.

it a forward movement that refuses to let history close in on itself. The prophets speak as if time is open, as if what is happening now is only part of a larger unfolding. Their words carry expectation, not only diagnosis. They stretch the listener beyond immediate circumstances into a horizon shaped by divine intention.

This forward-facing quality becomes one of the defining marks of prophetic imagination. It is not escape from reality, but a deeper engagement with it, where present suffering is placed within a larger trajectory of renewal.

Prophecy as Anticipation of Coming Transformation

Isaiah speaks into a fractured national condition with images that move beyond current instability. "The wilderness and the dry land shall be glad" (Isaiah 35:1), and "the glory of the Lord shall be revealed" (Isaiah 40:5). These statements do not describe present conditions; they anticipate transformation that has not yet arrived.

Jeremiah, even while describing destruction, holds a promise of future restoration: "I will restore the fortunes of my people Israel and Judah" (Jeremiah 33:7). The language moves forward even while describing collapse. Prophecy becomes a bridge between present brokenness and future renewal.

Ezekiel's vision of dry bones coming to life (Ezekiel 37:5–10) presents renewal not as gradual improvement but as divine re-creation. The image itself carries movement beyond what current reality can sustain.

Hope Beyond Present National Crisis

Prophetic voices often emerge during moments of national instability. Yet instead of being confined by crisis, they open a different horizon. Habakkuk begins with lament over injustice but ends with a posture of hope: "Though the fig tree should not blossom… yet I will rejoice in the Lord" (Habakkuk 3:17–18). The movement is not denial of crisis but reorientation within it.

Similarly, Isaiah speaks to a people facing exile with words that look beyond displacement: "Comfort, comfort my people" (Isaiah 40:1). The tone itself signals that present suffering is not the final frame of interpretation.

This hope is not abstract optimism. It is grounded in the conviction that history remains open under divine direction.

Vision of Restoration and Renewal

Restoration in prophetic literature is not limited to political return. It includes renewal of relationships, land, community life, and spiritual orientation. Amos envisions a day when "I will restore the fortunes of my people Israel" (Amos 9:14), where rebuilding includes agricultural stability and communal restoration.

Isaiah expands this vision further by describing a world where "they shall beat their swords into plowshares" (Isaiah 2:4). Conflict itself is reimagined within a transformed order of peace.

Even creation is included within restoration imagery. Isaiah speaks of new heavens and a new earth (Isaiah 65:17), where memory of former distress no longer defines existence.

Time Extended Beyond Immediate Political Reality

Prophetic imagination consistently extends time beyond immediate political cycles. Kings rise and fall, empires expand and collapse, yet prophetic vision continues beyond these patterns. Daniel's visions, for example, place earthly kingdoms within a larger sequence of historical unfolding (Daniel 7:13–14), where authority ultimately moves toward a different kind of rule.

This temporal extension reshapes how people understand their present moment. Life is no longer interpreted only through current rulers or immediate circumstances. It is placed within a longer narrative arc.

Joel's declaration that "I will pour out my Spirit on all flesh" (Joel 2:28) also reflects this extension, where future activity is envisioned beyond present limitations.

Direction Toward Unfolding Future History

The final movement of prophetic voice is directional. It does not only describe what will happen; it shapes expectation. Malachi ends with anticipation of preparation: "I will send my messenger, and he will prepare the way before me" (Malachi 3:1). The language opens forward rather than closing backward.

Zechariah speaks of nations coming to seek understanding of divine ways (Zechariah 8:22–23), placing future history within a shared movement of inquiry and response.

The prophetic horizon, therefore, is not static prediction but unfolding direction. It invites participation in a future that is still in motion.

A reflection in prophetic literature studies notes that "future orientation in the Hebrew prophets functions as a reconfiguration of historical time, where present crisis is interpreted within an open-ended trajectory of divine purpose."[35]

Conclusion

The prophetic movement does not stand apart from Israel's earlier story; it rises from within it. When national systems became stable yet internally strained, the prophetic voice entered as interruption. It did not simply add another layer of instruction but disturbed the rhythm of settled assumptions. Kingship, worship, and institutional life were brought into direct conversation with covenant memory. This interruption shaped how Israel understood its own direction, reminding the people that no structure could replace responsiveness to God's living word (Jeremiah 7:3–7).

Justice emerges as the central ethical concern within this prophetic reorientation. The prophets consistently reveal that worship detached from righteousness loses its meaning. "Let justice roll down like waters" (Amos 5:24) becomes more than a poetic expression; it defines the alignment expected between devotion and daily life. Ethical failure is not treated as a private matter but as a disruption within communal existence. The prophetic voice insists that how people treat one another becomes the visible measure of their faithfulness to God (Isaiah 1:16–17).

As this voice develops, its horizon expands beyond Israel's internal framework. Prophets speak of Egypt, Assyria, Babylon, and other nations not as outsiders to divine attention but as participants within it (Isaiah 19:23–25). The language of election is not removed, but it is reoriented toward inclusion. Israel's identity is repeatedly placed in relation to a wider human field, where other peoples are also drawn into divine awareness and future possibility. What begins as national correction gradually becomes global vision.

Within this widening scope, divine concern is consistently portrayed as comprehensive. Nations are evaluated, not only in terms of power or influence, but through justice, humility, and

---

[35] Rainer Albertz, "Time and Hope in the Prophetic Tradition of Ancient Israel," *Vetus Testamentum* 61, no. 3 (2011): 384.

responsibility before God (Micah 6:8). The prophetic tradition refuses to isolate moral accountability within a single group. Instead, it presents history itself as a shared moral space where human actions carry weight within a larger divine framework. This creates a worldview in which no nation exists outside the reach of ethical reflection and divine engagement.

The entire prophetic movement ultimately directs attention toward the future. Even when confronting present collapse or injustice, prophetic speech does not close history. It opens it. Visions of restoration, renewal, and transformed creation shape the imagination of the people (Isaiah 65:17–18). Time is extended beyond immediate political realities into a trajectory shaped by divine intention. The future becomes a space of expectation rather than closure.

Taken together, these movements form a coherent progression. Prophetic voice interrupts national systems. Justice becomes the central ethical concern. Vision expands beyond Israel. Divine concern includes all nations. History is directed toward future fulfillment. The narrative does not return to earlier cycles but continues forward, carrying the reader toward exile, restoration, and the widening scope of mission in the unfolding story of Scripture.

CHAPTER 8 — EXILE, DIASPORA, AND EXPANDED PRESENCE

The movement of the biblical narrative enters a profound transition when the stability of land, temple, and national structure gives way to displacement and dispersion. Exile marks a rupture in outward form, yet it does not signify the disappearance of identity. Instead, it becomes the setting in which vocation is carried beyond its traditional boundaries. What was once anchored in a single geographical center begins to unfold across multiple cultural and political environments, where continuity must now be sustained without territorial security.

Within this dispersed existence, identity is reshaped through presence rather than possession, and through faithfulness rather than location. Life among foreign nations becomes the new context in which meaning is carried forward, requiring wisdom, adaptation, and remembrance to sustain continuity. This chapter traces how exile transforms limitation into extension, where scattering does not end the narrative but redistributes it, allowing the people of God to exist as a living presence within the wider world.

Exile as Transition

The story of exile begins with a moment where everything that once gave visible stability comes to an end. The fall of Jerusalem is not only a political defeat but a collapse of an entire world of meaning. The city that carried memory, worship, and identity is broken as the Babylonians breach its walls and dismantle its structure (2 Kings 25:8–12). What remains is not only ruin but disorientation. The people who once oriented their lives around a visible center now find themselves without a geographical anchor.

This moment carries the weight of discontinuity. The rhythms of national life, the gatherings at the temple, and the visible symbols of belonging are no longer accessible. What was once experienced as permanence is now experienced as interruption. Yet even within this rupture, the narrative of

Scripture does not treat the event as abandonment. It becomes the beginning of a different form of continuity.

A historical parallel can be observed in the deportation practices of ancient empires, where conquered peoples were relocated to reduce resistance and encourage integration into imperial systems. Yet for Israel, this relocation becomes more than political strategy. It becomes a theological threshold where identity must survive without physical center.

Temple disruption and the silence of structure

The destruction of the temple carries a deeper symbolic weight than the loss of architecture. It represents the collapse of a structured way of encountering God that had shaped generations. The temple had functioned as the visible meeting point between divine presence and communal life. With its destruction, the people are forced to reimagine how relationship with God continues without a central sanctuary.

Psalmic reflection captures this inner displacement: "By the rivers of Babylon, there we sat down and wept when we remembered Zion" (Psalm 137:1). The memory of structured worship remains, yet it no longer corresponds to present reality. Songs once sung in stability now become expressions of longing within foreign land.

This silence is not absence of divine presence. It becomes the space where understanding begins to shift from location-based worship to presence that cannot be confined to architecture. The absence of the temple does not end the relationship; it reframes it.

Relocation into Babylonian life

The forced relocation into Babylon introduces a new environment where identity must be carried rather than displayed. Families, elders, scribes, and artisans are moved into a society with its own systems of governance, language, and cultural expectations (Jeremiah 29:1–7). Life continues, but within unfamiliar structures.

Yet within this displacement, a surprising instruction is given: to build, plant, and seek the welfare of the city where they now live. This direction reframes exile from pure loss into ongoing participation. The people are not instructed to disappear within the foreign system, nor to isolate themselves from it. They are called to inhabit it with purpose.

This moment marks a transition in understanding vocation. Identity is no longer tied to a single geographic expression but is carried into new environments. The people begin to learn that presence itself can become a form of continuity.

Loss reinterpreted as transition

Within exile, interpretation becomes essential for survival. Without reinterpretation, loss becomes finality. Yet the narrative gradually shifts toward understanding exile as transition rather than termination. The collapse of structures does not indicate collapse of divine intention.

This reorientation is reflected in prophetic reflection that continues within exile itself. The people are reminded that their story has not ended, only moved into another stage. The absence of land does not equate to absence of purpose. Instead, purpose begins to take a different form, one not dependent on geography.

A devotional rhythm begins to emerge within this reinterpretation. Memory becomes active rather than static. What was once anchored in place now becomes anchored in promise carried within community life.

Divine presence beyond territorial limits

One of the most profound shifts within exile is the realization that divine presence is not restricted to land-based systems. Earlier identity had been closely associated with temple-centered worship and national geography. In exile, this framework expands.

Even in Babylon, visions of divine activity continue to appear, as seen in Ezekiel's opening vision by the river Chebar (Ezekiel 1:1–3). The presence of God is encountered outside the expected location, signaling that displacement has not limited divine engagement. Instead, it has expanded the understanding of where presence can be known.

This realization does not remove grief, but it reshapes expectation. The people begin to understand that relationship with God travels with them. Identity is no longer dependent on a fixed center but on an enduring presence that accompanies them into dispersion.

From collapse to reformation

Exile, at its deepest level, becomes a transition from territorial identity to reformed identity carried within displacement. What appears as collapse becomes the beginning of redistribution. The center is no longer a place but a presence that moves with the people.

This transition does not erase memory; it transforms it into living continuity. The loss of Jerusalem becomes the beginning of a broader understanding of how identity survives beyond location. The people are no longer defined by where they stand, but by who remains with them in every place they go.

Life among Nations

Exile does not remain only a moment of loss. It becomes a way of living. What begins as displacement gradually turns into daily rhythm. The people who once lived within the boundaries of land, temple, and national order now find themselves learning how to exist inside the structures of another world. Life among nations begins not with choice but with circumstance, yet it quickly becomes the environment where identity is tested and carried forward.

Settling within imperial environments

The Babylonian context presents a structured and highly organized society. Young members of the displaced community are taken into royal service, trained in language, literature, and administrative practices of the empire (Daniel 1:1–7). Their names, education, and roles begin to reflect the expectations of the surrounding culture.

Yet within this structured assimilation, something deeper remains active. Identity is not erased; it is negotiated. The process is not only about learning new systems but about carrying inherited memory into those systems. Even when renamed and repositioned, continuity persists within internal conviction.

A quiet tension begins to shape daily life. Participation in imperial learning does not automatically mean surrender of identity. Instead, it becomes a space where loyalty is continually interpreted in practical decisions.

Negotiating heritage and survival

Life in exile requires constant negotiation between belonging and distinction. Participation in administrative roles offers stability, yet it also introduces pressure to conform. The question is no longer only about where they live, but how they live within what surrounds them.

Daniel and his companions represent this tension vividly. Their decision regarding food practices in Babylon is not merely dietary preference but a quiet act of identity preservation (Daniel 1:8–16). The choice is small in appearance, yet significant in direction. It signals that internal conviction continues even when external structures change.

Survival in exile does not remove heritage. Instead, it tests how deeply that heritage is embedded within ordinary decisions.

Faith within imperial systems

As life continues, presence within foreign systems becomes unavoidable. Administrative roles, public responsibilities, and social participation place the exiled community within the visible structure of empire. This visibility introduces both opportunity and tension.

Daniel's later experience in the royal administration shows how faith remains visible even at high levels of authority. His integrity becomes known within the system itself, shaping perception beyond private life (Daniel 6:3–5). What he carries inwardly begins to shape how he functions outwardly.

Faith is no longer expressed within temple courts or national gatherings. It is expressed within bureaucratic systems, public responsibility, and personal discipline.

Witness under exposure

The most defining moment of life among nations appears when private devotion becomes public exposure. The decree restricting prayer leads Daniel to continue his practice openly, facing consequences without altering rhythm (Daniel 6:10–13). His window remains open, not as defiance, but as continuity.

This moment shows how witness in exile is not constructed through territorial protection but through consistent practice. Faith becomes visible not because of isolation, but because of persistence within foreign structures.

The surrounding empire becomes the stage where identity is seen rather than hidden. What was once protected by land is now expressed through daily life under observation.

Presence carried through ordinary life

Life among nations gradually reshapes understanding of presence. It is no longer tied to location but to lived practice. Every decision, every interaction, and every act of integrity becomes part of how identity is expressed.

The shift is subtle but profound. Exile transforms witness from centralized worship into distributed presence. Identity is no longer guarded by boundaries but carried through participation.

The movement continues from loss of homeland into lived testimony within foreign space. Presence is no longer contained; it is enacted.

Identity in Foreign Context

Exile continues to reshape identity in a way that does not depend on geography. What once was secured through land, temple, and national visibility now begins to exist through memory, practice, and shared conviction. Belonging is no longer located in a single place. It is carried through people who continue to remember who they are even when surroundings no longer reflect it.

Covenant memory without land-based institutions

A defining shift occurs when identity is sustained without the physical frameworks that once supported it. The language of belonging no longer depends on temple systems or national administration. Instead, it is preserved through remembrance carried within the community itself.

Ezekiel captures this shift with clarity: "Yet I will be a sanctuary for them for a little while in the countries where they have gone" (Ezekiel 11:16). The presence once associated with a fixed place is now expressed within dispersion. Sanctuary is no longer confined to architecture but carried through divine relationship.

Identity begins to move from location to remembrance. What is remembered becomes what is preserved.

Identity shaped through narrative and practice

In foreign environments, identity is no longer reinforced by national rhythm. It is formed through repetition of memory, shared storytelling, and lived practices that continue across generations.

The community gathers identity through recounting what has been received. Psalmic reflection reveals this inner preservation: “By the rivers of Babylon we sat and wept when we remembered Zion” (Psalm 137:1–4). Memory is not passive recollection. It is active formation. Even lament becomes a form of continuity.

Practices such as prayer, ethical discipline, and communal gathering begin to function as anchors. Identity is carried through repeated actions that preserve belonging in unfamiliar surroundings.

Scripture and instruction as continuity

Instruction becomes a stabilizing force within displacement. What was once transmitted within structured national life now continues through instruction within dispersed communities. Learning becomes preservation. Memory becomes formation.

The words once spoken in land-based settings now circulate through oral repetition and written preservation. These texts and teachings do not merely inform belief. They sustain identity across distance.

Within this process, continuity does not depend on visibility of land but on constancy of remembrance.

Community formed in dispersion

Dispersed communities begin to recognize shared belonging even without shared territory. Gathering becomes intentional rather than geographical. Identity is reinforced through relational continuity rather than spatial unity.

Families and groups sustain belonging through shared practices, reinforcing that identity is not dissolved by displacement. Instead, it becomes distributed.

Belonging is no longer something located in one center. It is something carried together across multiple spaces.

Relational anchoring of identity

At the core of this transformation lies a deeper anchoring. Identity is no longer defined by political structure or geographic stability. It is rooted in relationship with God that remains active within dispersion.

The covenant memory does not fade with exile. It becomes internalized, shaping how people understand themselves even when external structures are absent.[36] Belonging continues because relationship continues.

Movement toward relational identity

The shift becomes clear. Identity moves from geographic definition to relational continuity. What once depended on land now depends on presence. What once depended on structure now depends on relationship. Exile does not erase identity. It relocates its center.

Wisdom and Adaptation

When identity is no longer protected by land or temple, it does not disappear—it learns to interpret reality differently. In exile, wisdom is not merely intellectual reflection; it becomes survival shaped by attentiveness to God within unfamiliar systems. The book of Daniel opens this inner world clearly. In Babylon, where imperial power defines knowledge and authority, Daniel receives understanding not as personal genius but as something "given" from God who "gives wisdom to the wise and knowledge to those who have understanding" (Daniel 2:20–23). This shifts wisdom away from institutional certainty into lived dependence.

Wisdom in exile is therefore not detached thinking. It is perception formed under pressure. It learns to read political structures without being absorbed by them. It learns to serve without surrendering identity. Babylon becomes both classroom and testing ground. Within it, faith does not retreat; it becomes alert, responsive, and interpretive. The mind of faith begins to operate within complexity rather than outside it.

Ethical negotiation in imperial space

Exile does not remove moral tension; it intensifies it. The story of Esther reveals how survival and identity must often be negotiated within systems that do not share covenant memory. In the Persian court, invisibility could mean safety, but silence could also mean collapse. When crisis arrives, Mordecai's challenge reframes her position: deliverance may come, but responsibility cannot be avoided (Esther 4:13–16). The moral weight of presence becomes unavoidable.

---

[36] Mark W. Hamilton, *"Memory, Identity, and Exilic Community Formation in Ezekiel,"* Journal for the Study of the Old Testament 44, no. 2 (2019): 287.

What emerges here is not rigid separation from culture, but discernment within it. Esther remains inside the system while refusing to let it define her ultimate loyalty. Wisdom in exile learns how to move carefully through political space without losing ethical clarity. It is neither withdrawal nor assimilation; it is awareness shaped by belonging to a deeper story than empire.

Identity preserved through practice

In Babylon, identity is not maintained through geography but through repeated practices that resist erosion. Daniel's refusal to compromise at the table of the king is not about food alone; it is about memory embodied in daily life (Daniel 1:8–16). Small decisions become carriers of larger belonging. Faith is preserved not in declarations alone, but in patterned living.

This form of adaptation does not weaken identity; it stabilizes it. Repetition of prayer, dietary discipline, and interpretive dependence on God become the structure through which continuity survives displacement. Identity is not defended by isolation but maintained through consistent embodied practice within foreign space.

Discernment in public and private life

Exile creates dual pressure: public integration and private loyalty. Daniel's life shows how these two spaces remain connected without contradiction. He participates in administrative responsibility under imperial authority, yet his private rhythm of prayer remains directed toward Jerusalem (Daniel 6:10–13). This is not hidden rebellion; it is structured fidelity.

Discernment becomes the essential skill of survival. Not every structure is rejected, but not every structure is neutral. Wisdom must decide what participation looks like without dissolving identity. The challenge is not simply cultural presence but faithful interpretation of that presence.

Adaptation as faithful presence

Across exile life, adaptation does not mean compromise of vocation. It means sustaining identity in unfamiliar conditions. The people of God learn that faith is not dependent on location; it is carried through memory, practice, and relationship with God.

Psalmic lament captures this tension with raw honesty: "By the rivers of Babylon we sat and wept when we remembered Zion" (Psalm 137:1–4). Memory here is not nostalgia alone; it is resistance against forgetting who they are. Even in displacement, identity refuses to dissolve.[37]

Adaptation becomes faithful presence when it holds memory and engagement together. The community does not lose direction in foreign space; it learns to carry direction within foreign space.

Presence without Territory

The experience of exile introduces a profound shift in how divine presence is understood within the life of the community. What was once closely associated with land, temple, and centralized worship begins to be encountered within dispersed and unfamiliar environments. The vision recorded in Ezekiel emerges "by the Kebar River among the exiles" (Ezekiel 1:1–3), and this setting becomes the interpretive point where presence is no longer confined to geography but encountered within displacement itself.[38] In this moment, divine engagement is not interrupted by exile but revealed through it, showing that movement away from land does not result in the withdrawal of divine presence but in its reconfiguration within history.

This shift reshapes the meaning of belonging. Identity is no longer experienced through proximity to a fixed center but through continuity of relationship carried into scattered life. What was once assumed to be tied to sacred space begins to be understood as sustained within lived experience. The community learns that presence is not restricted by location but remains active within movement, allowing identity to endure even when external structures collapse.

Life within foreign systems

The instruction given to the exiles by Jeremiah deepens this understanding by redefining how life is to be lived in foreign contexts. The call to build houses, plant gardens, and seek the welfare of the city where they reside (Jeremiah 29:4–7) introduces

---

[37] Smith, Mark S. *The Origins of Biblical Monotheism: Israel's Polytheistic Background and the Ugaritic Texts*. Oxford: Oxford University Press, 2001, p. 172.

[38] Daniel L. Smith-Christopher, "Reassessing the Social Location of the Babylonian Exile," *Journal for the Study of the Old Testament* 56, no. 2 (1992): 67.

a pattern of engagement rather than withdrawal. Life in exile is not framed as passive survival but as active participation within the structures of foreign societies. This reorientation transforms displacement into a space of presence rather than absence.

Within this setting, daily life becomes the primary location of witness. Faith is no longer expressed primarily through centralized worship but through patterns of living within unfamiliar environments. Work, relationships, and ethical conduct begin to carry the weight of identity. The community does not disappear into the surrounding culture, nor does it isolate itself from it. Instead, it inhabits foreign systems while maintaining continuity of belonging, allowing presence itself to become a form of vocation.

Continuity in dispersion

As exile continues, continuity is preserved not through territorial stability but through memory, shared identity, and communal practices that sustain belonging across distance. The absence of centralized structures does not dissolve identity but relocates it within the lived experience of dispersed communities. Belonging is carried through narrative, instruction, and collective memory rather than institutional form.

This form of continuity reveals that identity can remain stable even when geography changes. The people are no longer defined by access to a single location but by their participation in a shared story that transcends place. What emerges is a form of unity that is sustained through relational and experiential continuity rather than spatial concentration. Identity becomes mobile without becoming fragmented, maintaining coherence within dispersion.

Presence as vocation

Within this dispersed condition, presence itself becomes the expression of vocation. To exist faithfully among nations is to embody identity through lived existence rather than territorial possession. The scattered community learns that calling is not diminished by displacement but redefined through it. Purpose is carried within life itself, allowing identity to be expressed wherever the people are found.

This reorientation does not represent the loss of direction but the transformation of how direction is lived. Presence becomes the means through which vocation is sustained across multiple contexts. The people of God are no longer defined by where they are located but by how they exist within the world around them. Identity is carried through presence rather than protected by boundaries.

Conclusion

Exile reconfigures the meaning of loss by transforming it into a transition of identity rather than an end of purpose. What appears as disruption of national life becomes the setting in which identity is carried forward in a new form. The collapse of familiar structures does not cancel divine direction but relocates it within lived displacement. The people who once understood themselves through land and centralized institutions begin to recognize continuity within scattering, where identity is no longer protected by geography but sustained through relationship and memory.

Life among nations becomes the primary context in which this transformed identity is expressed. Daily existence within foreign systems becomes the arena of witness, where faith is no longer confined to inherited spaces but embodied through participation in diverse cultural environments. The ordinary rhythms of life, work, and interaction become the means through which continuity is maintained. Witness emerges not through separation from surrounding cultures but through faithful presence within them, allowing identity to be seen through conduct rather than location.

Within this dispersed reality, identity is sustained without dependence on a geographic center. The absence of a unified homeland does not dissolve belonging but redefines its foundation. Belonging is no longer anchored in proximity to a single sacred site but in continuity of relationship that travels with the people across boundaries. The community remains coherent not because of territorial stability but because of shared memory, practice, and recognition of divine faithfulness within history.

Wisdom becomes essential for sustaining this form of life, enabling faithful adaptation within complex and shifting environments. It shapes discernment in public and private spheres, allowing the community to engage surrounding systems without losing continuity of identity. Adaptation does not mean dilution of vocation but careful navigation of presence within multiple cultural frameworks. Through wisdom, survival becomes meaningful participation rather than mere accommodation, preserving integrity within dispersion.

Presence ultimately replaces territory as the defining marker of mission. What once depended on land and centralized worship is now carried through existence itself. Identity is expressed through how the people live within the world rather than where they reside. Mission is no longer contained within a fixed location but distributed across diverse contexts, where presence itself becomes the sign of continuity and purpose.

This chapter establishes exile not as collapse of divine purpose but as redistribution of presence across nations. The movement shifts from land-centered identity to dispersed yet continuous vocation, where identity is carried through life rather than secured by place. The narrative prepares for themes of restoration and return, while also opening toward a broader horizon in which mission is understood as globally distributed presence rather than geographically bounded structure.

CONCLUSION—ISRAEL, HISTORY, AND UNFINISHED MISSION

The movement that has unfolded from calling through covenant, redemption, law, settlement, monarchy, prophetic interruption, and exile reveals a narrative that consistently resists closure within any single stage. Israel's identity emerges not as a static achievement, but as a dynamic participation within a larger unfolding purpose that moves through history itself. Each phase contributes meaning, yet none is presented as final completion, suggesting that the story is intentionally structured as ongoing rather than concluded.

As the narrative reaches this point of reflection, what becomes clear is that history itself functions as the medium through which divine purpose continues to advance. The people of Israel remain within this movement, not as an isolated endpoint, but as part of a trajectory that extends beyond their own historical boundaries. This conclusion gathers the entire sequence into a single perspective, where calling, failure, restoration, and dispersion are understood as interconnected movements within an unfinished mission that continues to point beyond itself.

Israel as Instrument Within History

The entire movement of Israel's story, when viewed from its beginning in Abraham's calling to its later dispersion among the nations, reveals a consistent pattern where identity is never self-generated but received, shaped, and directed. The starting point was never self-definition, but interruption. "Go from your country, your people and your father's household to the land I will show you" (Genesis 12:1). From that moment onward, identity is carried as response rather than possession. Israel does not begin with a settled idea of itself, but with a summons that places it into motion within history. That motion becomes the defining shape of its existence.

Across the unfolding narrative, Israel consistently functions as a carrier of something larger than itself. In Egypt, it is carried through oppression toward deliverance (Exodus 3:7–

10). In the wilderness, it becomes a community learning dependence rather than independence (Deuteronomy 8:2–3). In the land, it becomes a people tested by stability and distraction (Judges 2:10–12). Under monarchy, it becomes a structured nation wrestling with power and responsibility (1 Samuel 8:4–7). Through prophetic correction, it becomes a people continually recalled to its original direction (Isaiah 1:16–17). Even in exile, it becomes a dispersed presence carrying memory into foreign spaces (Jeremiah 29:4–7). At every stage, the pattern remains consistent: Israel is positioned within history as a vessel through which a wider purpose is unfolding.

This positioning clarifies a distinction that runs quietly but persistently through the entire narrative: the difference between instrument and endpoint. Israel is never presented as the final horizon of its own story. It is instead placed within a trajectory that consistently moves beyond itself. Covenant does not close in on national completion; it opens outward into responsibility. Law does not end in cultural consolidation; it forms a way of life that reflects divine character. Kingship does not resolve identity; it exposes both strength and fracture. Prophetic speech does not affirm closure; it reopens direction. Exile does not end presence; it redistributes it across new contexts. Each stage resists finality within Israel itself, pointing instead toward something beyond its immediate frame.

What becomes visible across this movement is continuity of purpose that does not depend on stability of structure. Even when institutions shift, collapse, or reform, the underlying direction remains intact. The promise spoken to Abraham about blessing extending to "all peoples on earth" (Genesis 12:3) does not disappear within later historical developments. It reappears in covenant structure, in legal formation, in prophetic vision, and in dispersion among the nations. The thread remains unbroken, even when the form changes. This continuity suggests that Israel's historical function is not dependent on geographic permanence or institutional strength, but on participation in an ongoing movement that exceeds each individual stage.

At the same time, the narrative consistently extends beyond ethnic or national limitation. From the earliest promise, the horizon includes nations outside Israel's immediate boundary.

Egypt becomes the place of revelation, not only oppression. Assyria and Babylon become instruments within the larger narrative, not external interruptions to it. Prophets speak to surrounding nations as part of their message (Amos 1:3–5). Exile places Israel directly within foreign systems, where its presence becomes interwoven with other peoples rather than isolated from them (Jeremiah 29:5–7). This repeated expansion indicates that Israel's role is never self-contained. It is always relational, always outward-facing, always embedded within a wider human field.

When viewed in this way, Israel's identity is best understood not as a closed category but as a functional presence within history. It carries memory, it preserves calling, it endures failure, and it continues through change, but none of these elements exist for self-closure. They exist as part of a larger movement that consistently moves beyond Israel toward a broader horizon. The story does not terminate within national identity. It moves through it.

Mission Moving Through History

The story that has unfolded from Abraham to exile does not move as a set of isolated ideas placed on top of history. It moves inside history itself. Each stage of Israel's journey is not a separate theological category but a lived moment shaped by decisions, environments, crises, and encounters. Mission, in this sense, is never suspended above reality. It is always happening within it.

From the moment Abraham leaves Ur, the narrative is already embedded in geography, movement, and uncertainty (Genesis 12:1–4). The calling does not arrive as an abstract principle but as a disruption of settled life. That pattern continues as the descendants move into Egypt, where survival becomes the space in which divine promise is remembered and tested (Genesis 46:3–4). The exodus does not occur in symbolic terms but within political oppression, economic systems, and imperial structures (Exodus 1:11–14; Exodus 3:7–10). The wilderness period is not conceptual training but lived dependence shaped by hunger, guidance, conflict, and provision (Exodus 16:2–5). Each moment is historical, concrete, and irreversible.

As the narrative progresses into settlement, monarchy, and prophetic engagement, the same pattern continues. Covenant is not an idea floating above society; it is lived within tribal organization, agricultural life, and national tension (Joshua 24:14–18). Law is not detached instruction; it is embedded in family structures, justice systems, and communal responsibility (Deuteronomy 15:7–11). Kingship arises within political pressure and social expectation rather than theoretical design (1 Samuel 8:19–20). Prophetic voices emerge inside courts, marketplaces, and public crisis points, addressing real decisions and real consequences (2 Samuel 12:7–9; Amos 5:10–12). Even exile is not an interruption of mission but a new historical environment in which identity continues under foreign rule (Jeremiah 29:4–7).

Across all these movements, one pattern remains consistent: divine purpose does not bypass history but moves through it. Human decisions are never erased, nor are they ignored. They become part of the unfolding narrative. Failure becomes part of the record, just as obedience does. Instability does not stop direction; it becomes the context in which direction is reasserted. This interaction between divine intention and human participation is not theoretical but historical, shaped through real events and consequences.

Mission, therefore, cannot be understood apart from time. It is not a parallel reality running alongside human history. It is expressed through the very texture of historical existence itself. Empires rise and fall, communities form and dissolve, leaders succeed and fail, but within all of this movement, a consistent trajectory continues. The story is carried forward not by abstraction but by lived experience.

What emerges is a unified vision of history as the primary medium through which mission is revealed. Every stage of Israel's journey becomes part of a continuous narrative, where calling, covenant, failure, correction, and restoration are not separate themes but interwoven expressions of one unfolding purpose.

Tension Between Calling and Failure

The narrative of Israel does not move in a straight line of success or collapse. It carries both at the same time, often within the same generation, sometimes within the same leader. Calling remains present, but it does not erase instability. Failure appears repeatedly, but it does not cancel the underlying purpose that began with Abraham. The story holds these realities together without separating them into different categories.

From the beginning, this tension is already visible. Abraham is called, yet he struggles with fear in Egypt (Genesis 12:10–13). Jacob carries promise, yet his path is marked by conflict and deception (Genesis 27:18–24). The people who emerge from Egypt are delivered, yet they resist trust in the wilderness (Exodus 16:2–3). Even after entering the land, cycles of faithfulness and failure continue across generations (Judges 2:11–19). These are not interruptions in the story; they are part of its actual movement.

Monarchy and fracture within unity

With the rise of monarchy, the tension becomes even more visible in structured national life. Saul is chosen, yet his leadership reflects instability and disobedience (1 Samuel 13:13–14). David carries both devotion and moral failure within the same narrative arc (2 Samuel 11:2–4; 2 Samuel 12:7–10). Solomon's wisdom coexists with gradual compromise that affects national direction (1 Kings 11:4–6). The kingdom itself begins to reflect internal division, where unity and fracture exist side by side (1 Kings 12:16–19).

Prophetic voices do not remove this tension. Instead, they expose it while still affirming that the story has not ended. Elijah confronts covenant breakdown on Mount Carmel, yet the narrative continues beyond confrontation (1 Kings 18:21–39). Amos speaks against injustice while still assuming that the people remain within the scope of divine attention (Amos 5:21–24). Isaiah speaks judgment and hope within the same historical environment, holding both realities together (Isaiah 1:18–20; Isaiah 6:8–13).

Exile as consequence and continuation

Exile becomes the clearest expression of this tension. It is both consequence and continuation. The people experience displacement, yet they are not erased from the story (2 Kings 25:8–12). Jeremiah speaks of judgment, but also of continued purpose in foreign land (Jeremiah 29:4–7). Ezekiel sees both collapse and renewal in vision, holding destruction and restoration within one horizon (Ezekiel 11:16–17).

Even in exile, failure does not cancel identity, and calling does not prevent consequence. Instead, both remain present within the same historical frame. The people are scattered, yet they remain part of an ongoing narrative that has not lost direction.

Holding contradiction without resolution

What becomes clear across this entire movement is that the narrative refuses to simplify itself. It does not resolve tension by removing failure or by redefining calling as something abstract. Both remain visible at the same time. This coexistence becomes one of the defining features of the story.

In later reflection on ancient Israel's development, Mark S. Smith describes how Israel's identity tradition preserves contradiction rather than eliminating it, allowing failure and vocation to remain interwoven within the same historical memory.[39] This observation aligns with what the narrative itself already demonstrates: continuity is not maintained by perfection but by persistence of purpose within imperfection.

The tension therefore is not a flaw in the story. It is part of how the story moves forward. Calling continues to exist within instability, and instability continues to exist within calling, without either one ending the other.

Nations as Constant Horizon

From the earliest movement of the narrative, the story is never contained within a single people speaking only to themselves. The call given to Abraham already carries an outward direction that resists closure. The promise is not only about formation of a family, but about influence extending beyond it, where "all peoples on earth will be blessed" (Genesis 12:3). That sentence alone quietly reshapes the entire direction of what follows, because it introduces the nations not as background, but as part of the intended horizon of the story itself.

Even before Israel becomes a structured nation, the surrounding world is already shaping the narrative. Egypt is not a distant reference point but the place where identity is tested under pressure (Genesis 41:57). Babylon is not only an ending point of crisis but a space where memory and faith are reinterpreted in

---

[39] Mark S. Smith, *The Early History of God: Yahweh and the Other Deities in Ancient Israel* (Grand Rapids: Eerdmans, 2002), 312.

exile (2 Kings 25:11–12). Assyria appears not as a side detail but as an active force shaping the language of prophetic warning and interpretation (Isaiah 10:5–6). These empires are not interruptions to the story; they are part of how the story is understood.

Prophetic speech beyond borders

As the narrative develops, the prophetic tradition begins to address nations directly. This is not occasional expansion but consistent movement outward. Egypt is spoken to in judgment and warning (Isaiah 19:1). Babylon is named in both critique and limitation of power (Isaiah 13:1–5). Tyre, Edom, Moab, and other surrounding nations are included within the scope of prophetic attention (Amos 1:3–5; Ezekiel 25:1–7). The language assumes that divine engagement is not restricted to one political identity.

Jonah's story intensifies this pattern in a different direction. The prophet is sent specifically to Nineveh, a foreign city, and his struggle reveals the difficulty of accepting that divine concern extends beyond expected boundaries (Jonah 3:1–4). Yet the narrative moves toward Nineveh's response, showing that repentance is not geographically limited (Jonah 3:10). The text quietly expands the horizon of moral accountability beyond Israel's internal world.

Life in displacement and shared space

When exile becomes historical reality, the presence of nations is no longer external; it becomes daily environment. In Babylon, life unfolds within imperial systems, administrative structures, and cultural negotiation (Daniel 1:3–5). Yet even within this setting, identity continues to express itself through loyalty, practice, and conviction (Daniel 6:10–13). Jeremiah's instruction to the exiles to "seek the peace and prosperity of the city" where they live (Jeremiah 29:7) reveals that engagement with foreign space is not accidental but part of ongoing vocation.

This movement shows that the people of God do not exist outside the world of nations; they exist within it at every stage. Egypt, Assyria, Babylon, Persia, and surrounding regions are not marginal locations but formative environments. Identity is shaped through interaction, pressure, and adaptation within these contexts.

Horizon that never closes

What becomes clear is that the narrative never develops into a closed internal system. It begins with nations in view, continues through national interaction, and ends in dispersion among multiple cultural worlds. The presence of nations is not an addition to the story; it is part of its original architecture.

In historical reflection on ancient Israel's development, Israel's identity cannot be understood without its consistent engagement with surrounding nations, since its vocation is framed within a world already populated by diverse peoples. This observation highlights what the narrative itself repeatedly demonstrates: the story is always lived at the intersection between one people and many nations.

The horizon therefore remains open throughout. From calling to covenant, from monarchy to exile, the nations remain present not as background detail but as continuous reference point. The story never turns inward completely, because it was never designed to remain within itself.

Transition Toward Fulfillment Beyond Israel

Across the long movement of the narrative, there are moments when the structures that once carried identity begin to feel insufficient to contain what is being revealed. Monarchy provides order, yet also exposes fracture (1 Kings 12:16–19). Temple-centered worship gives focus, yet becomes vulnerable to displacement and loss (2 Kings 25:9–10). Even covenant life, though foundational, is lived within repeated cycles of tension between faithfulness and failure (Judges 2:18–19). These structures are not rejected, but they are shown to be part of a larger movement that cannot be fully contained within them.

This does not signal collapse of meaning. It signals movement beyond fixed expression. The story continues to unfold in ways that stretch the boundaries of national, political, and institutional form. What begins in a single household with Abraham gradually expands through land, law, monarchy, prophecy, and exile, until it can no longer be described as only an internal national narrative.

Prophetic horizon widening the frame

Within this development, prophetic speech consistently refuses to allow the story to settle into finality. Isaiah speaks of a light extending beyond Israel into nations that were previously outside direct covenant identity (Isaiah 49:6). Micah envisions a time when multiple peoples stream toward a shared center of divine instruction (Micah 4:1–2). Malachi speaks of a future where reverence is not geographically confined but acknowledged among diverse peoples (Malachi 1:11). These images do not close the narrative; they stretch it forward.

Even exile contributes to this widening. The scattering of the people across multiple regions does not erase identity but disperses it into new environments where presence continues without centralized form (Jeremiah 29:5–7). The story begins to move in a direction where location is no longer the defining boundary of vocation.

Redistribution rather than conclusion

Exile does not function as an ending point in the narrative logic. Instead, it becomes a form of redistribution. Identity is carried into multiple cultural spaces, and meaning is no longer tied to a single geographic center. The people of God exist within Babylon, Persia, and later broader imperial settings, not as an interruption of purpose but as continuation in altered form (Daniel 1:3–6).

This shift suggests that fulfillment is not located within one historical structure. It is moving through and beyond those structures. The narrative does not terminate at the restoration of land or the rebuilding of institutions. Even when return occurs, the sense of completion remains open-ended, pointing toward something not yet fully realized within the historical frame.

Toward a wider unfolding

The trajectory that begins in calling continues through covenant, land, monarchy, prophetic correction, and exile, but it does not resolve within any of these stages. Each stage contributes, yet none contains the final shape of what is being formed. The movement consistently points outward and forward. The biblical narrative consistently resists closure within Israel's historical experience, instead shaping expectation toward a fulfillment that transcends national boundaries while still carrying Israel's story within it. This insight aligns with the way the narrative itself unfolds, where every stage contributes to a larger movement without becoming its final form.

The conclusion of this trajectory is not termination but anticipation. The story remains intentionally unfinished within its own historical boundaries, preparing for a continuation that will carry its themes into a wider and more complete horizon of fulfillment.

Conclusion

Across the entire unfolding narrative, Israel consistently appears not as an end in itself but as an instrument within a wider movement that extends beyond its own boundaries. From the initial calling of Abraham (Genesis 12:1–3), through covenant formation, through redemption from Egypt, through law, monarchy, prophetic correction, and finally exile, the identity of the people is shaped through participation rather than possession. At no point does the narrative settle into self-contained completion. Each stage points beyond itself, suggesting that what is formed is always serving a larger unfolding purpose.

This means that Israel's significance is real, but never isolated. It is always relational, always directional, always embedded within a broader horizon that continues to expand as the story progresses.

History as the space of divine engagement

The movement of the narrative is consistently grounded in history rather than abstraction. Divine purpose is not presented as detached from human experience but expressed through concrete events, political shifts, cultural pressures, and social transformation. The journey from Egypt (Exodus 12:41), the settlement in the land (Joshua 21:43–45), the rise and fragmentation of monarchy (1 Kings 12:19), the prophetic interventions during crisis (Isaiah 6:8–11), and the experience of exile (2 Kings 25:11–12) all demonstrate that history itself becomes the medium through which meaning unfolds.

Nothing in the narrative exists outside historical texture. Even moments of spiritual significance are carried within real environments shaped by conflict, displacement, and restoration. The story advances through time, not outside it.

Persistent tension within calling

One of the defining features that remains unresolved throughout the narrative is the tension between calling and failure. The people are consistently described as chosen, yet repeatedly marked by instability. Faithfulness and unfaithfulness coexist within the same historical movement (Judges 2:11–19). Leadership structures rise and collapse. Covenant memory is preserved and forgotten in alternating cycles. Prophetic voices speak into both renewal and resistance.

This tension is not resolved within the narrative itself. Instead, it is carried forward as part of the identity formation process. Calling does not eliminate failure, and failure does not cancel calling. Both remain active within the unfolding story, shaping its complexity rather than simplifying it.

Nations as continuous presence

From the earliest stages of the narrative to its later dispersion, nations remain a constant horizon. They are present in promise, in conflict, in prophetic engagement, and in exile. Egypt shapes the memory of deliverance (Exodus 1:11–14). Assyria and Babylon shape the language of judgment and displacement (Isaiah 10:5–6; Jeremiah 25:11). Surrounding nations are addressed within prophetic imagination, and later become the lived environment of dispersed communities (Daniel 1:1–5).

This continuity shows that the narrative is never confined internally. It always exists in relation to a wider human world, where identity is shaped through interaction rather than isolation.

Movement toward what lies beyond

The overall trajectory of the narrative does not conclude within its own historical boundaries. Instead, it remains intentionally open, moving toward fulfillment that exceeds the structures it has developed. Covenant, law, monarchy, prophecy, land, and exile all contribute to formation, yet none of them complete the story. Each becomes part of a larger forward movement that resists closure.

The direction of the narrative is therefore forward-facing rather than static. It moves through history without ending within it, carrying expectation of fulfillment that lies beyond itself, while still preserving continuity with everything that has come before.

Final movement of the narrative

What emerges across this entire progression is a unified yet unfinished movement. Israel functions within mission, not as its final goal. History becomes the space of divine engagement rather than background setting. Calling and failure remain in sustained tension rather than resolution. Nations remain present throughout every stage rather than appearing as secondary detail. And the entire narrative remains open, moving toward fulfillment beyond itself.

This movement preserves continuity from beginning to end while refusing closure within any single stage. It holds together identity, history, and purpose in a forward-moving framework that naturally extends beyond its own boundaries.

Explore Related Books

Thank you for reading this book. It is my prayer that these pages have strengthened your faith, deepened your understanding of God's Word, and encouraged your walk with Jesus Christ.

All my writings are born out of a desire to explore Scripture deeply and to address important theological and practical questions faced by believers today. I have authored nearly 100 spiritually enriching and scholarly books covering Biblical Theology, Missions, Evangelism, Christian Living, Discipleship, Biblical Psychology, Comparative Religion, Family Life, and in-depth Scriptural studies. These writings are designed to strengthen faith, deepen biblical understanding, answer important theological questions, and equip believers for faithful Christian living in today's world.

To explore more books and resources, please visit the official website:

www.venkatpotana.com

There you will find additional books organized by topic to support your continued spiritual learning journey. New books are being added regularly, and this growing collection is intended to serve believers over time with expanding biblical and theological resources. All books are available for convenient online purchase in print, eBook, PDF, and audiobook formats through trusted platforms such as Amazon, Pothi, Google Play, and other global distributors.

www.ingramcontent.com/pod-product-compliance
Ingram Content Group UK Ltd.
Pitfield, Milton Keynes, MK11 3LW, UK
UKHW021401190726
13845UKWH00028B/816

9 788168 665439